GREAT ESCAPES OF WORLD WAR II

TUNNELING TO FREEDOM

THE GREAT ESCAPE FROM STALAG LUFT III

by Nel Yomtov

CAPSTONE PRESS
a capstone imprint

3 9082 11750 5175

Graphic Library is published by Capstone Press,
1710 Roe Crest Drive, North Mankato, Minnesota 56003
www.mycapstone.com

Library of Congress Cataloging-in-Publication Data
Names: Yomtov, Nelson, author. | Valdrighi, Alessandro, illustrator.
Title: Tunneling to freedom : the great escape from Stalag Luft III / by Nel Yomtov ; illustrated by
    Alessandro Valdrighi.
Other titles: Great escape from Stalag Luft III
Description: North Mankato, Minnesota : Capstone Press, [2017] | Series: Graphic library. Great escapes of
    World War II | Audience: Grades 4–6. | Audience: Ages 8–14.
Identifiers: LCCN 2016040416| ISBN 9781515735311 (library binding) | ISBN 9781515735366 (paperback) |
    ISBN 9781515735489 (ebook : .pdf)
Subjects: LCSH: Stalag Luft III—Comic books, strips, etc.—Juvenile literature. | Prisoner-of-war escapes—Comic
    books, strips, etc.—Juvenile literature. | Prisoners of war—United States—Comic books, strips, etc.—
    Juvenile literature. | World War, 1939–1945—Prisoners and prisons, German—Comic books, strips, etc.—
    Juvenile literature.
Classification: LCC D805.P7 Y66 2017 | DDC 940.54/7243812—dc23
LC record available at https://lccn.loc.gov/2016040416

Summary: In graphic novel format, follows the incredible story of the brave men who tunneled to freedom from
Stalag Luft III, a German prisoner-of-war camp, during World War II.

Editor
Christopher Harbo

Art Director
Nathan Gassman

Designer
Ted Williams

Media Researcher
Wanda Winch

Production Specialist
Gene Bentdahl

Illustrator
Alessandro Valdrighi

Design Elements: Shutterstock: aodaodaodaod,
paper texture, esfera, map design,
Natalya Kalyatina, barbed wire design

Printed and bound in the United States of America.
10042S17

TABLE OF CONTENTS

PRISONERS OF THE NAZIS

During World War II (1939–1945), Allied forces flew thousands of bombing missions over Germany and Nazi-occupied territory in Europe. The goal of the missions was to knock out railways, harbors, factories, and oil resources. Almost any enemy activity that helped the German war effort was a target for the Allied bombers.

Allied airmen, however, faced stiff resistance from the Germans. Speedy, well-armed German fighter planes, as well as guns positioned on the ground, shot down many Allied aircraft. Those Allied pilots lucky enough to survive being blasted out of the sky and crashing to the ground were captured by German soldiers as prisoners of war.

The captured Allied airmen were sent to prison camps. Prison life was grim, and every prisoner, or *kriegie*, knew he faced possible death. One of the most famous camps was known as Stalag Luft III. A "Stalag Luft" was a prisoner-of-war camp specially built for downed enemy airmen.

ESCAPE PLAN
TOM
DICK
HARRY
GEORGE
THEATRE
KITCHENS
COAL STORE
COOLER
HOSPITAL
ROADWAY
GERMAN GUARD
123
107
106
122
108
105
121
104
120
110
103
119
101

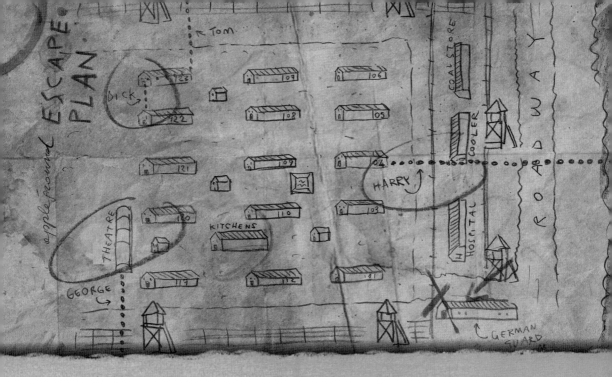

Stalag Luft III was run by the Nazi air force. Opened in May 1942, the camp was built to hold Allied officers. It was located near the town of Sagan, about 100 miles (160 kilometers) southeast of Berlin.

Most notably, Stalag Luft III was very secure. The Nazis even claimed the camp was "escape-proof." Tunneling out of Stalag Luft III was difficult because the soil was sandy. In addition, the Nazis had placed sound detectors in the ground to learn of any tunneling activities. German guards armed with machine guns kept watch on the prisoners from tall towers overlooking the camp.

Although escape seemed impossible, dozens of tunnel attempts were made at Stalag Luft III by spring 1943. Every attempt failed. Still, every prisoner was committed to escaping. As the months wore on, the prisoners' plans of escape became ever more bold and courageous. The time was ripe for a plan to finally succeed.

BREAK OUT!

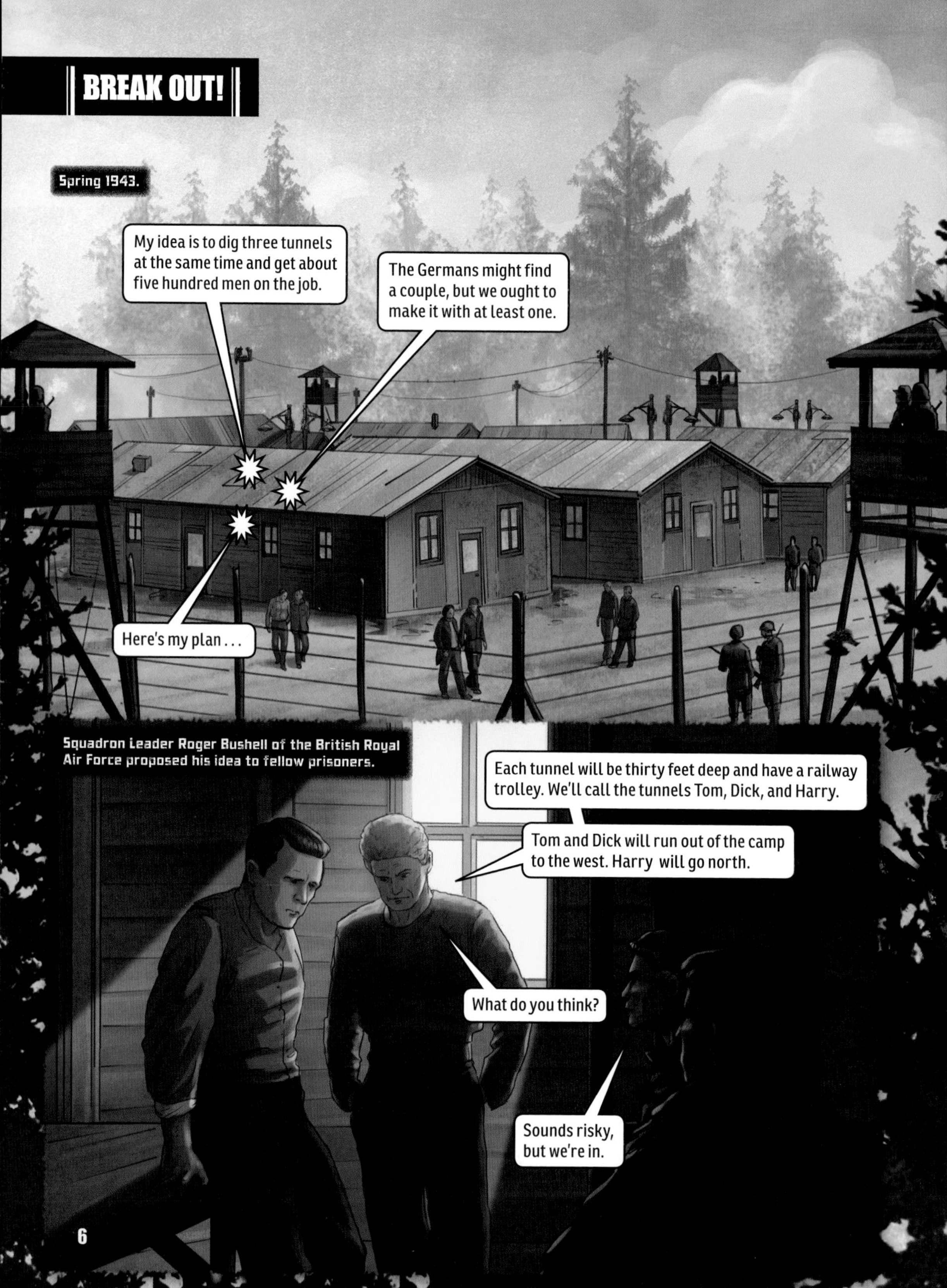
Spring 1943.
My idea is to dig three tunnels at the same time and get about five hundred men on the job.
The Germans might find a couple, but we ought to make it with at least one.
Here's my plan . . .
Squadron Leader Roger Bushell of the British Royal Air Force proposed his idea to fellow prisoners.
Each tunnel will be thirty feet deep and have a railway trolley. We'll call the tunnels Tom, Dick, and Harry.
Tom and Dick will run out of the camp to the west. Harry will go north.
What do you think?
Sounds risky, but we're in.

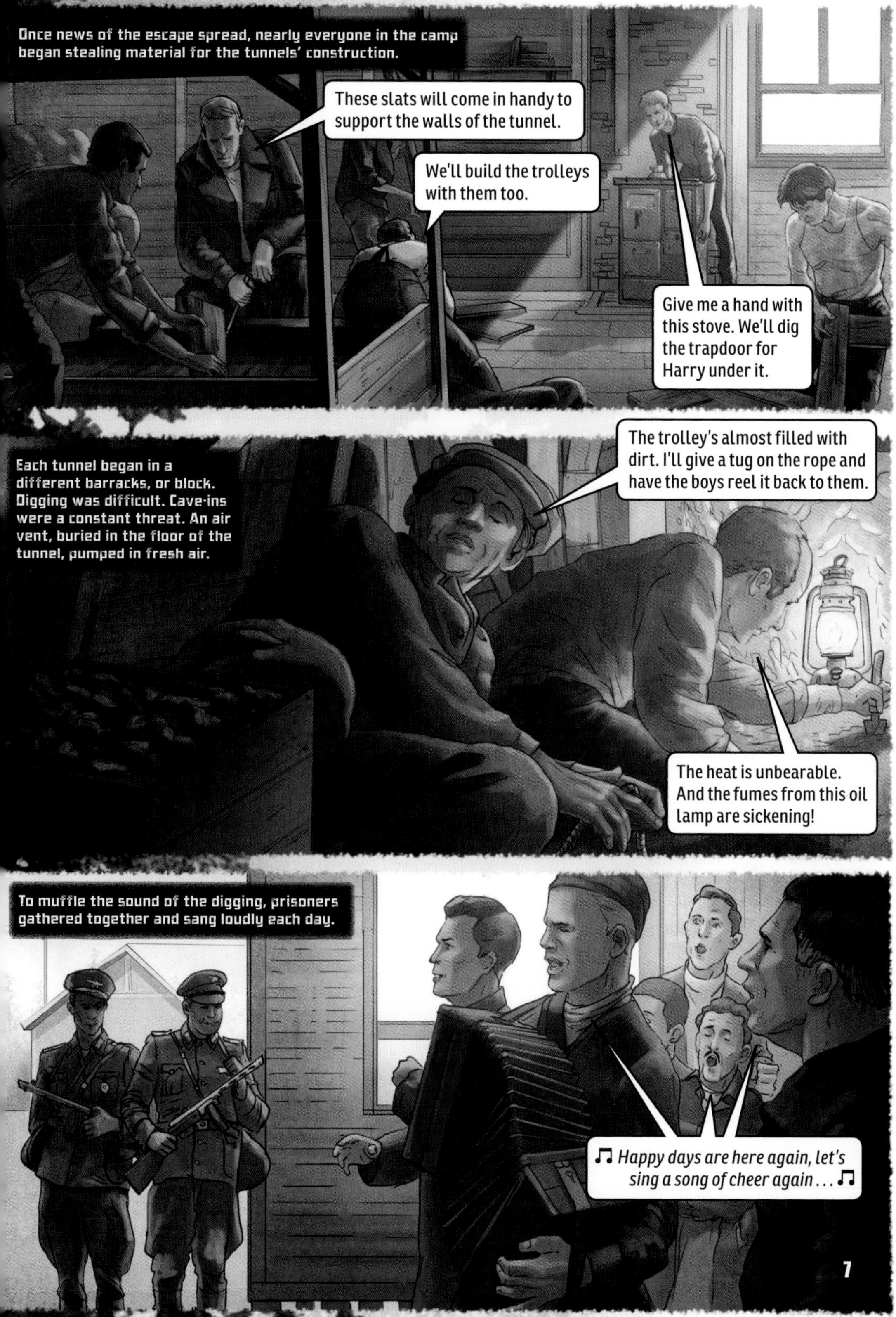
Once news of the escape spread, nearly everyone in the camp began stealing material for the tunnels' construction.
These slats will come in handy to support the walls of the tunnel.
We'll build the trolleys with them too.
Give me a hand with this stove. We'll dig the trapdoor for Harry under it.
Each tunnel began in a different barracks, or block. Digging was difficult. Cave-ins were a constant threat. An air vent, buried in the floor of the tunnel, pumped in fresh air.
The trolley's almost filled with dirt. I'll give a tug on the rope and have the boys reel it back to them.
The heat is unbearable. And the fumes from this oil lamp are sickening!
To muffle the sound of the digging, prisoners gathered together and sang loudly each day.
♫ *Happy days are here again, let's sing a song of cheer again . . .* ♫

The dirt taken from the tunnels was put into cloth bags that were worn inside pant legs. When the men pulled a string, the bag opened and the dirt fell out onto the ground.

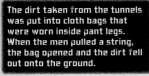

"Factories" were set up to produce the material needed once the men escaped.

A forgery department created new identities for each escapee. Letters and passes were forged to allow the men to travel through Nazi territories.

The tailoring department was run by Tommy Guest and Ivo Tonder. Most of the tailors were Czech and Polish air force officers.

Nice work on that suit, Ivo.

Thanks, Tommy. That German uniform will pass for the real thing too.

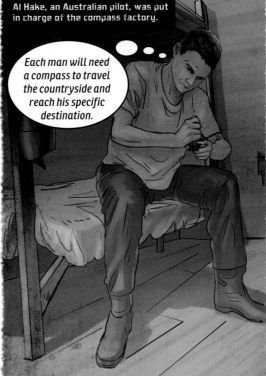

Al Hake, an Australian pilot, was put in charge of the compass factory.

Each man will need a compass to travel the countryside and reach his specific destination.

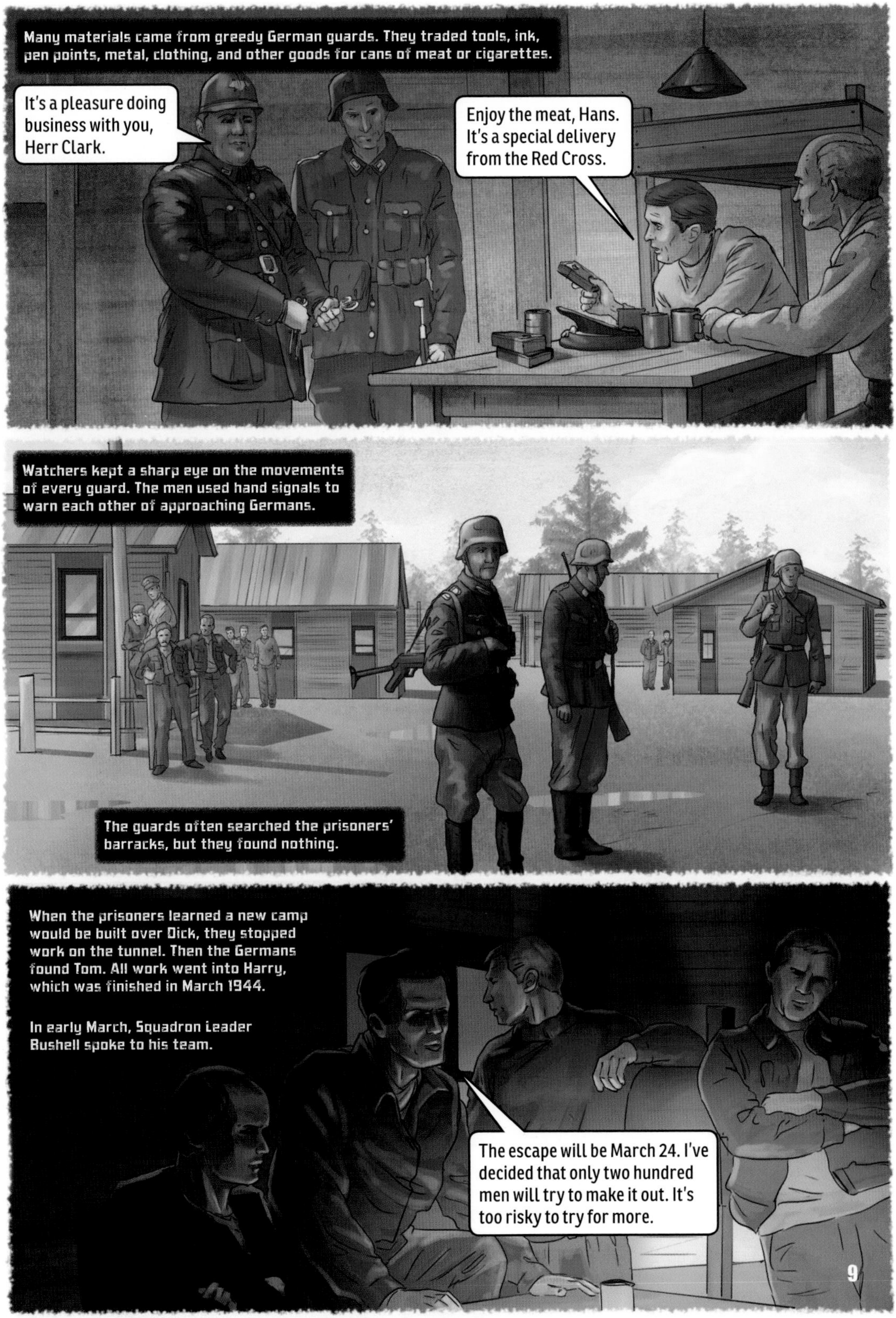
Many materials came from greedy German guards. They traded tools, ink, pen points, metal, clothing, and other goods for cans of meat or cigarettes.
It's a pleasure doing business with you, Herr Clark.
Enjoy the meat, Hans. It's a special delivery from the Red Cross.
Watchers kept a sharp eye on the movements of every guard. The men used hand signals to warn each other of approaching Germans.
The guards often searched the prisoners' barracks, but they found nothing.
When the prisoners learned a new camp would be built over Dick, they stopped work on the tunnel. Then the Germans found Tom. All work went into Harry, which was finished in March 1944.
In early March, Squadron Leader Bushell spoke to his team.
The escape will be March 24. I've decided that only two hundred men will try to make it out. It's too risky to try for more.

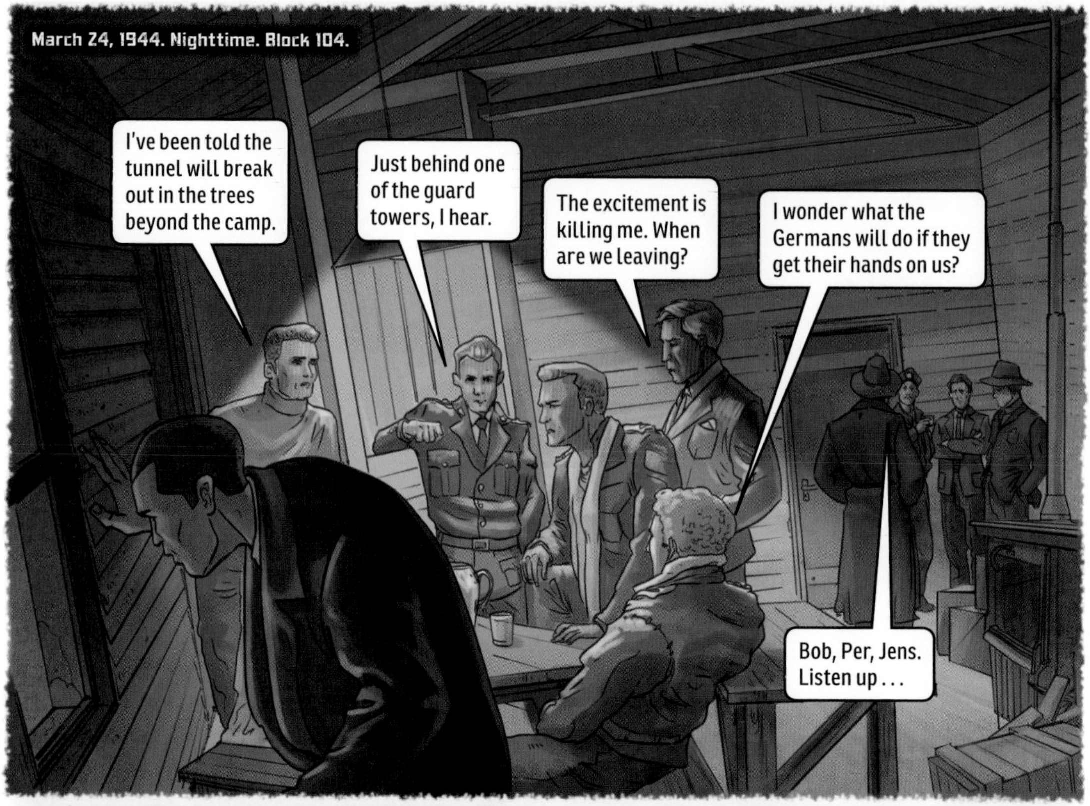
March 24, 1944. Nighttime. Block 104.
I've been told the tunnel will break out in the trees beyond the camp.
Just behind one of the guard towers, I hear.
The excitement is killing me. When are we leaving?
I wonder what the Germans will do if they get their hands on us?
Bob, Per, Jens. Listen up . . .

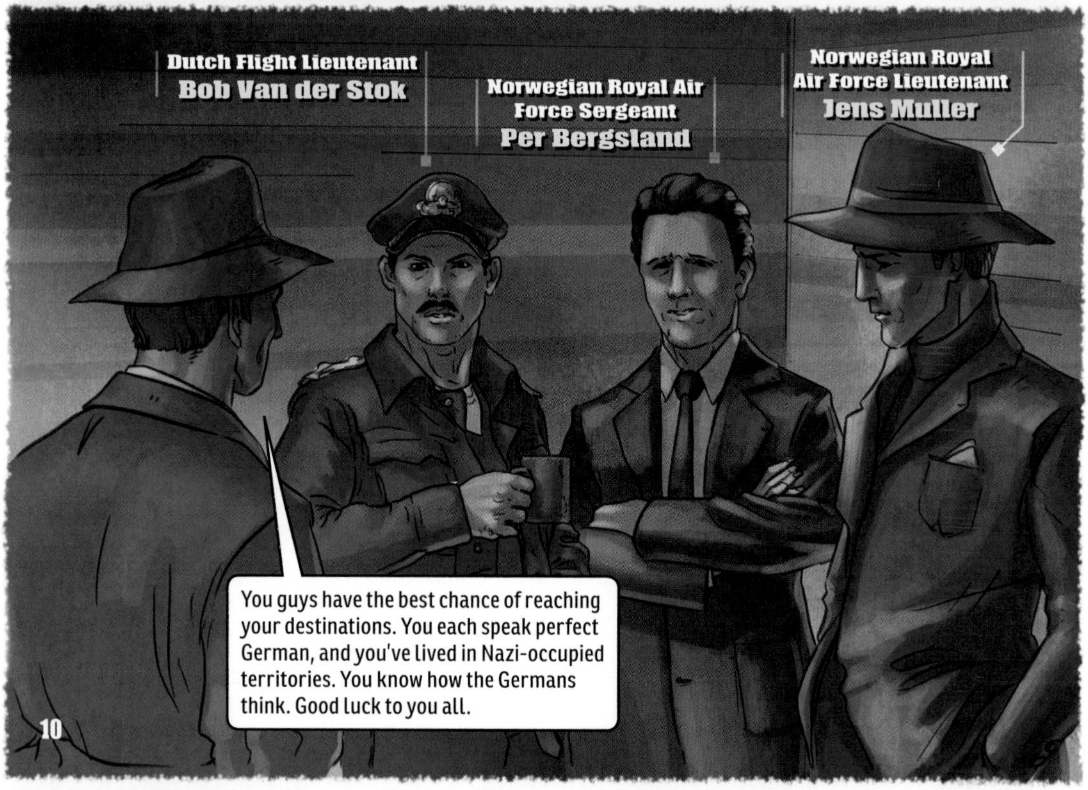
Dutch Flight Lieutenant
Bob Van der Stok
Norwegian Royal Air Force Sergeant
Per Bergsland
Norwegian Royal Air Force Lieutenant
Jens Muller
You guys have the best chance of reaching your destinations. You each speak perfect German, and you've lived in Nazi-occupied territories. You know how the Germans think. Good luck to you all.

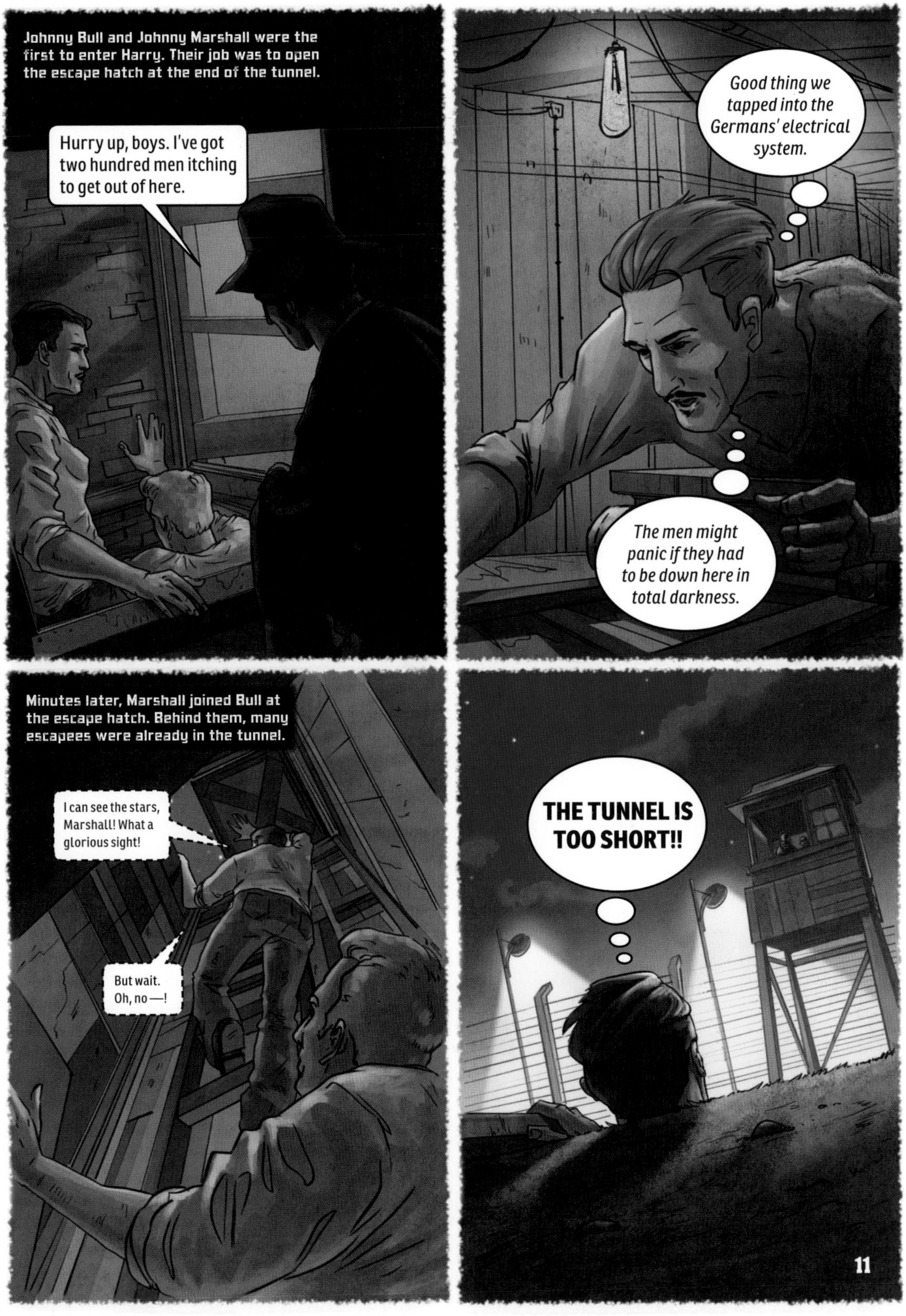
Johnny Bull and Johnny Marshall were the first to enter Harry. Their job was to open the escape hatch at the end of the tunnel.
Hurry up, boys. I've got two hundred men itching to get out of here.
Good thing we tapped into the Germans' electrical system.
The men might panic if they had to be down here in total darkness.
Minutes later, Marshall joined Bull at the escape hatch. Behind them, many escapees were already in the tunnel.
I can see the stars, Marshall! What a glorious sight!
But wait. Oh, no —!
THE TUNNEL IS TOO SHORT!!

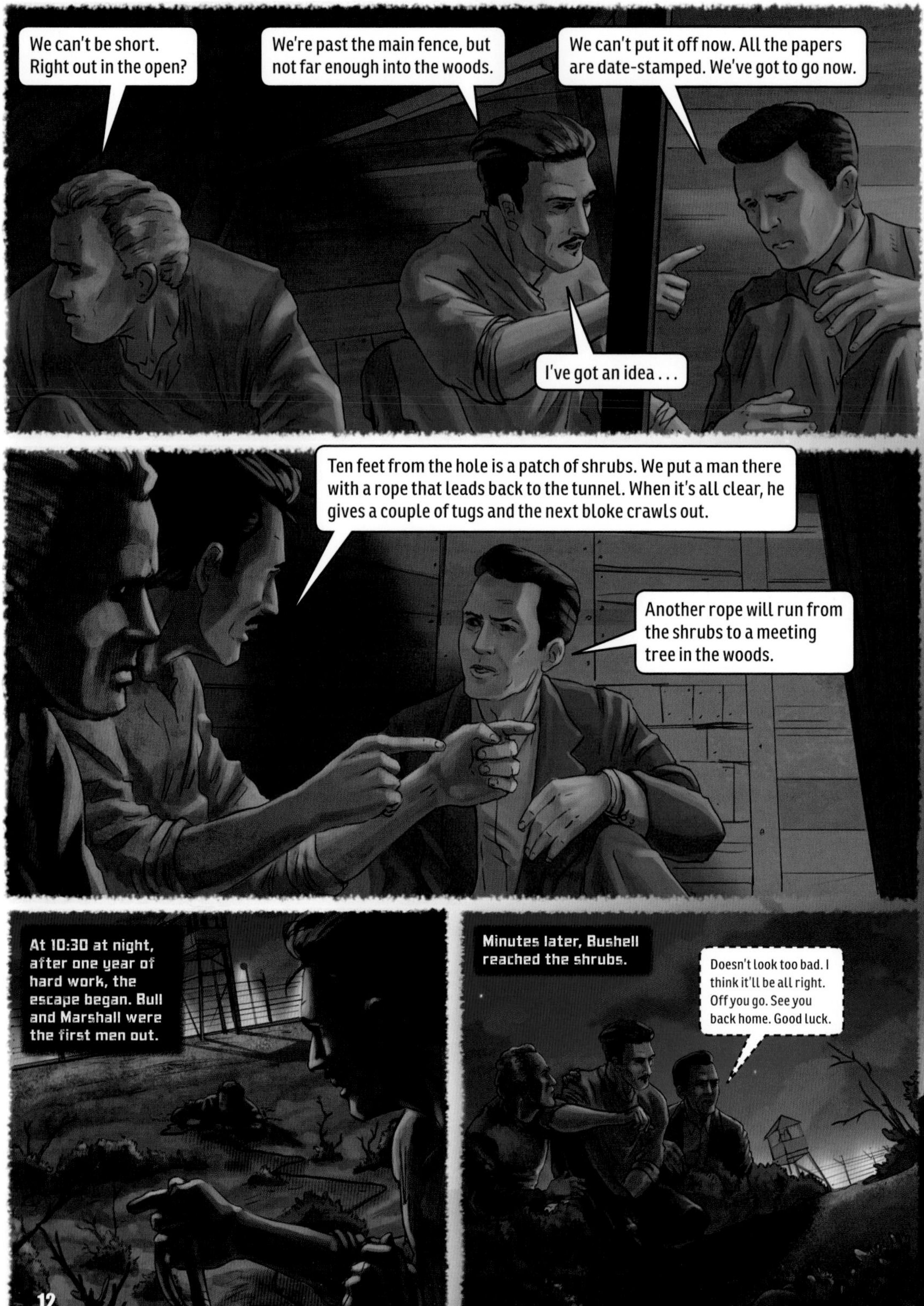

We can't be short. Right out in the open?
We're past the main fence, but not far enough into the woods.
We can't put it off now. All the papers are date-stamped. We've got to go now.
I've got an idea . . .
Ten feet from the hole is a patch of shrubs. We put a man there with a rope that leads back to the tunnel. When it's all clear, he gives a couple of tugs and the next bloke crawls out.
Another rope will run from the shrubs to a meeting tree in the woods.
At 10:30 at night, after one year of hard work, the escape began. Bull and Marshall were the first men out.
Minutes later, Bushell reached the shrubs.
Doesn't look too bad. I think it'll be all right. Off you go. See you back home. Good luck.

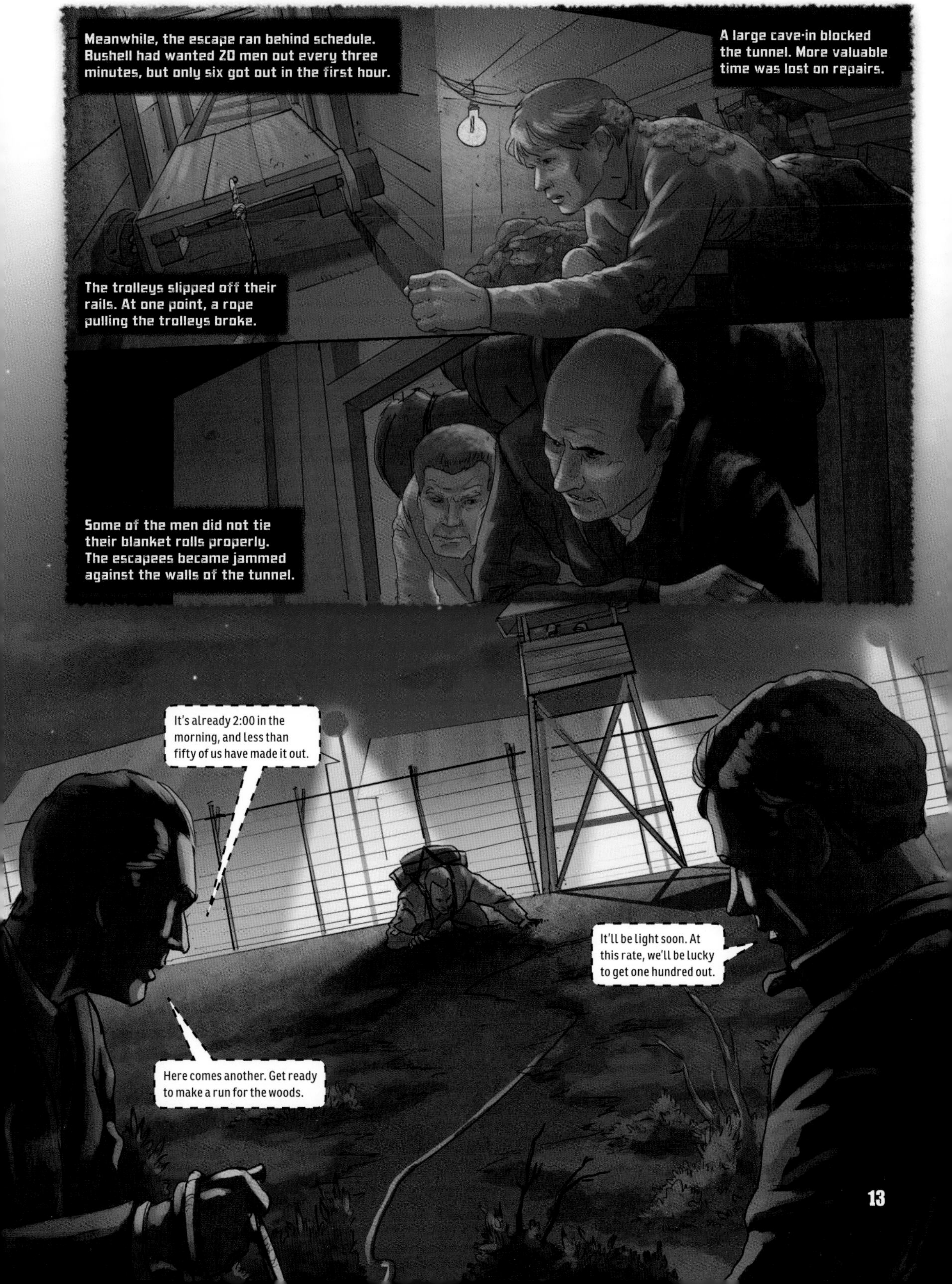

Meanwhile, the escape ran behind schedule. Bushell had wanted 20 men out every three minutes, but only six got out in the first hour.
A large cave-in blocked the tunnel. More valuable time was lost on repairs.
The trolleys slipped off their rails. At one point, a rope pulling the trolleys broke.
Some of the men did not tie their blanket rolls properly. The escapees became jammed against the walls of the tunnel.
It's already 2:00 in the morning, and less than fifty of us have made it out.
It'll be light soon. At this rate, we'll be lucky to get one hundred out.
Here comes another. Get ready to make a run for the woods.

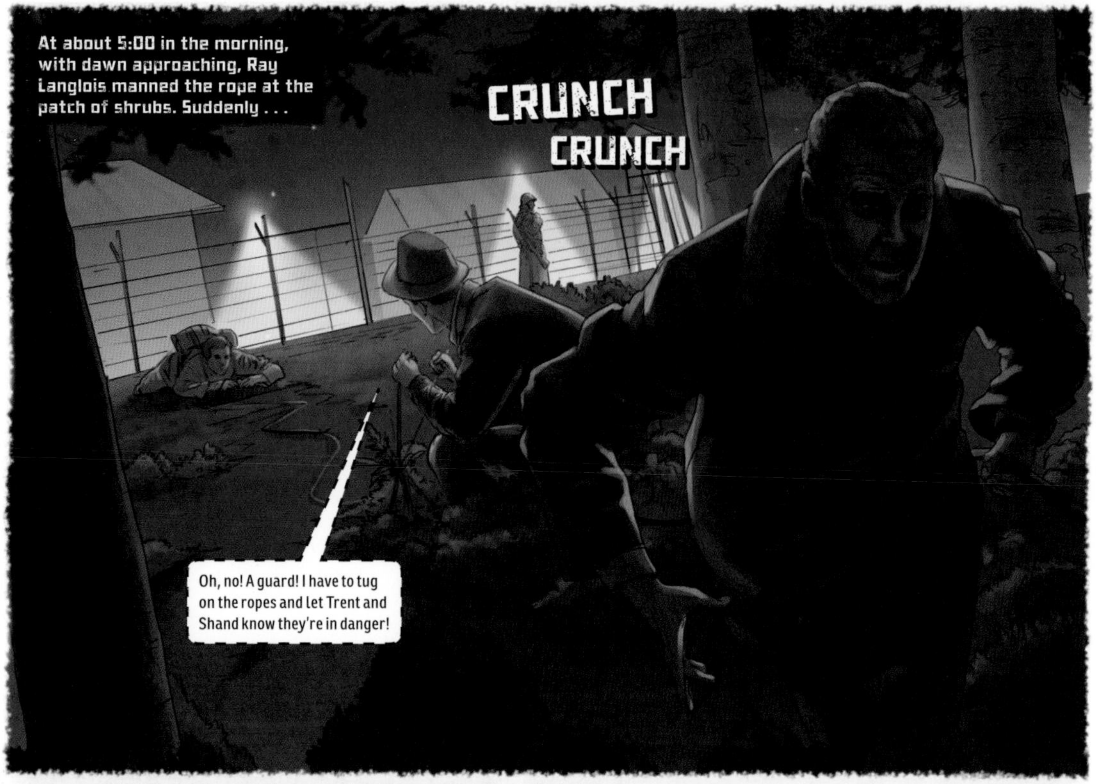
At about 5:00 in the morning, with dawn approaching, Ray Langlois manned the rope at the patch of shrubs. Suddenly . . .
CRUNCH
CRUNCH
Oh, no! A guard! I have to tug on the ropes and let Trent and Shand know they're in danger!

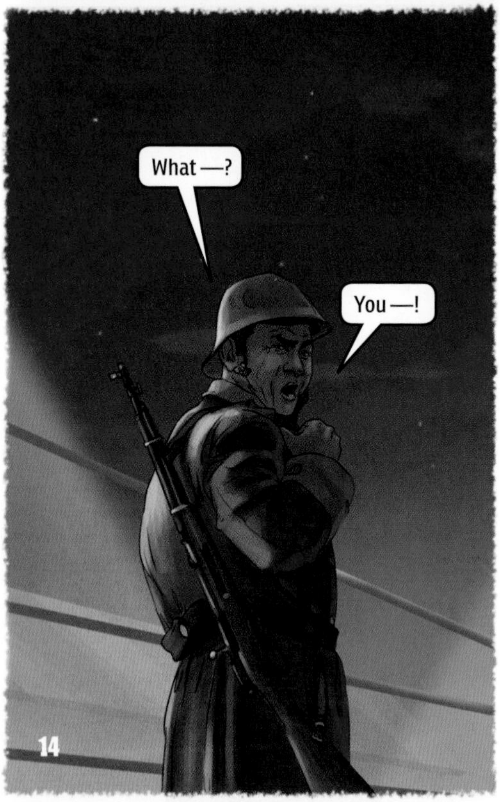
What —?
You —!

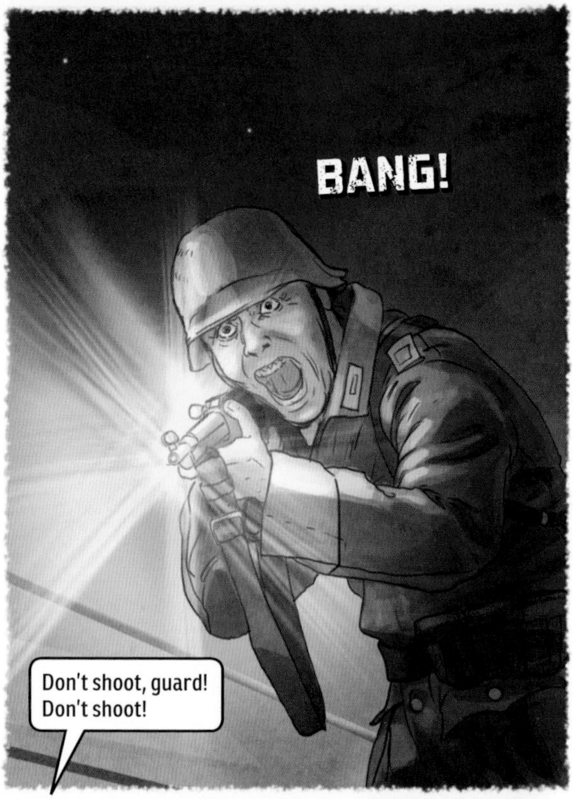
BANG!
Don't shoot, guard! Don't shoot!

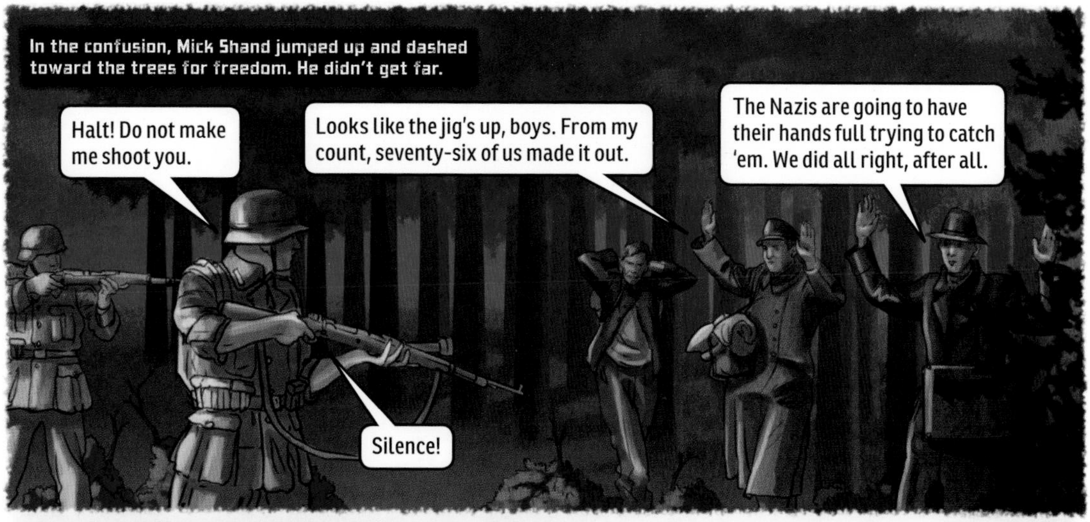
In the confusion, Mick Shand jumped up and dashed toward the trees for freedom. He didn't get far.
Halt! Do not make me shoot you.
Looks like the jig's up, boys. From my count, seventy-six of us made it out.
The Nazis are going to have their hands full trying to catch 'em. We did all right, after all.
Silence!

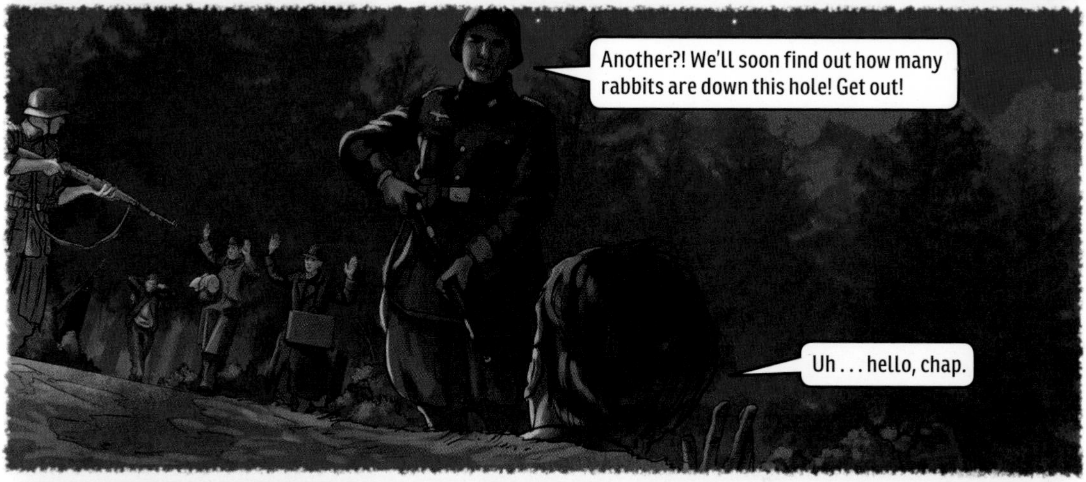
Another?! We'll soon find out how many rabbits are down this hole! Get out!
Uh . . . hello, chap.

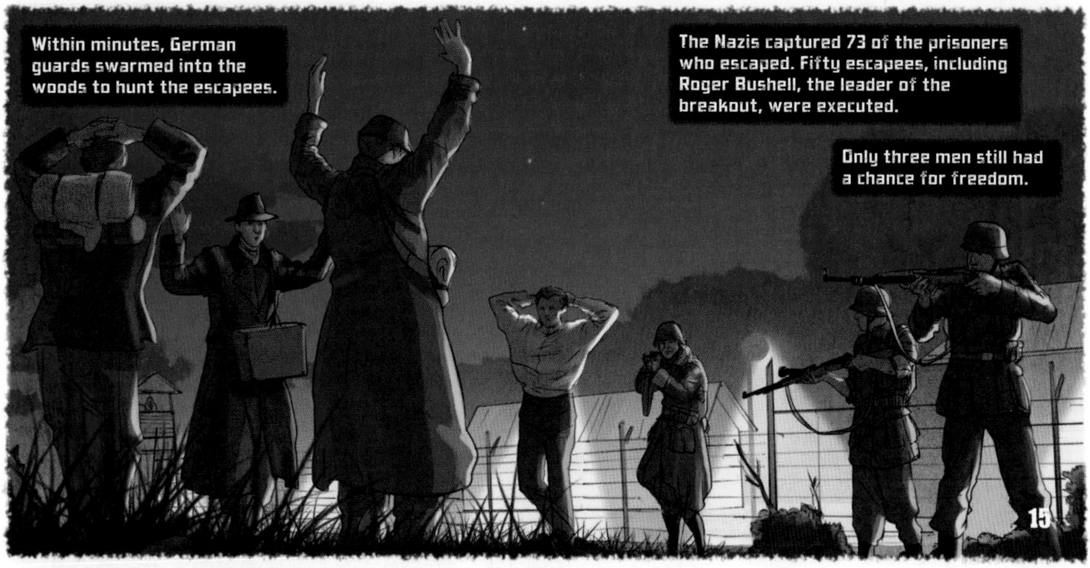
Within minutes, German guards swarmed into the woods to hunt the escapees.
The Nazis captured 73 of the prisoners who escaped. Fifty escapees, including Roger Bushell, the leader of the breakout, were executed.
Only three men still had a chance for freedom.

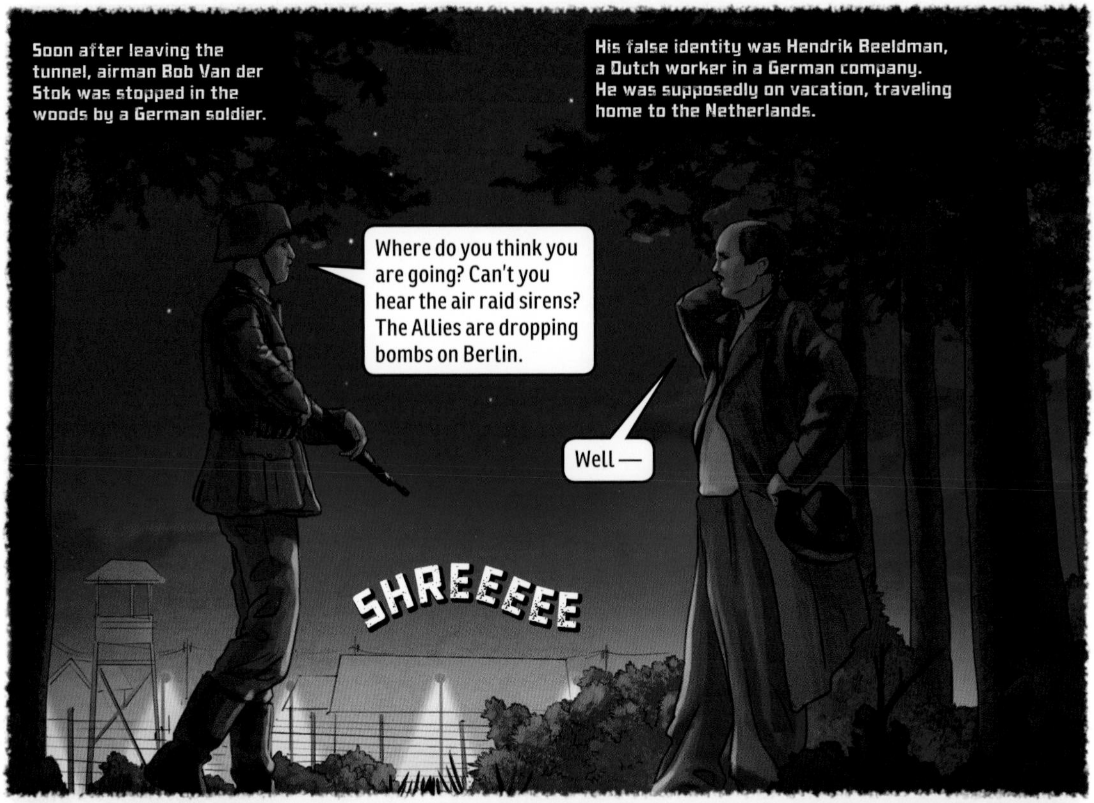
Soon after leaving the tunnel, airman Bob Van der Stok was stopped in the woods by a German soldier.
His false identity was Hendrik Beeldman, a Dutch worker in a German company. He was supposedly on vacation, traveling home to the Netherlands.
Where do you think you are going? Can't you hear the air raid sirens? The Allies are dropping bombs on Berlin.
Well —
SHREEEEE

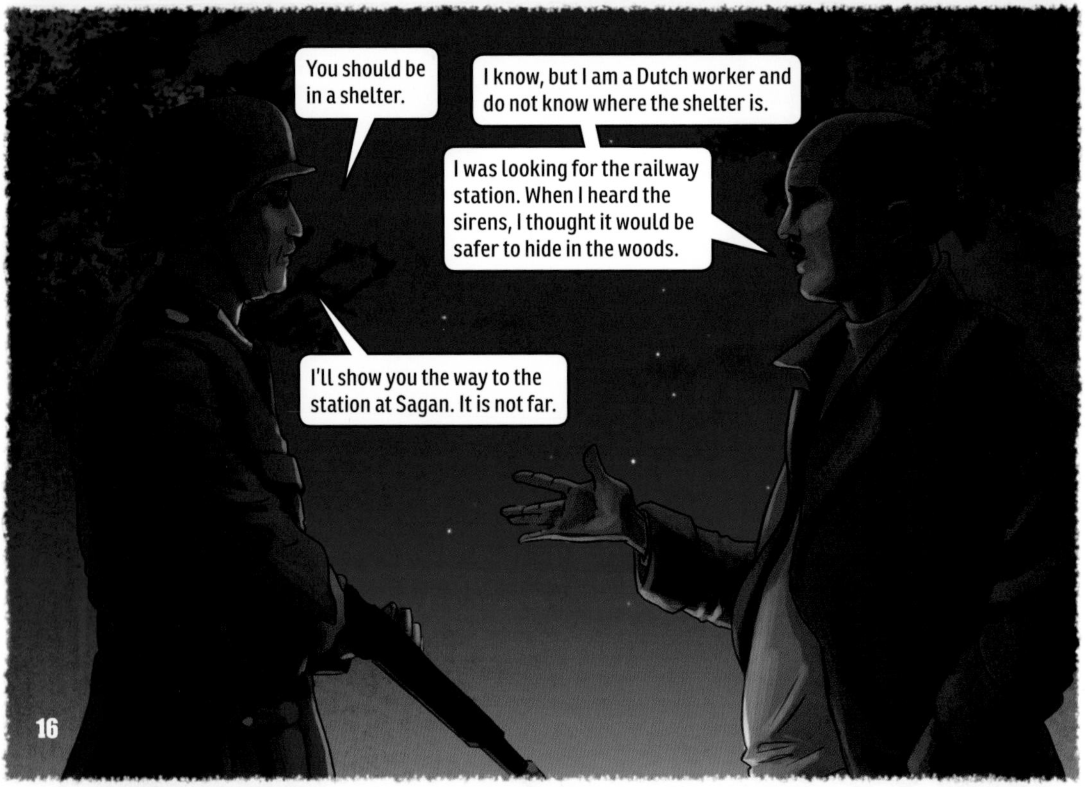
You should be in a shelter.
I know, but I am a Dutch worker and do not know where the shelter is.
I was looking for the railway station. When I heard the sirens, I thought it would be safer to hide in the woods.
I'll show you the way to the station at Sagan. It is not far.

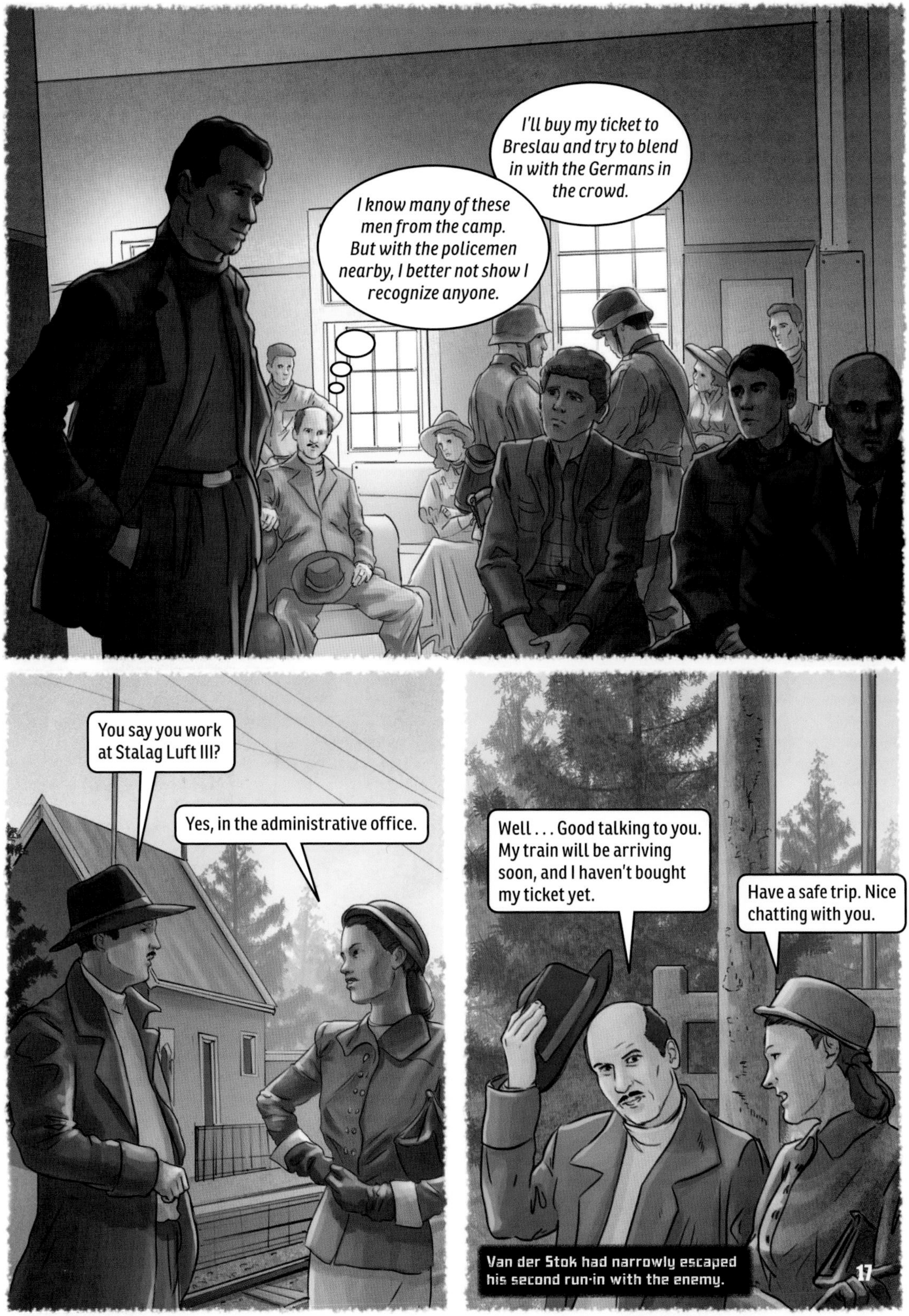
I'll buy my ticket to Breslau and try to blend in with the Germans in the crowd.
I know many of these men from the camp. But with the policemen nearby, I better not show I recognize anyone.
You say you work at Stalag Luft III?
Yes, in the administrative office.
Well . . . Good talking to you. My train will be arriving soon, and I haven't bought my ticket yet.
Have a safe trip. Nice chatting with you.
Van der Stok had narrowly escaped his second run-in with the enemy.

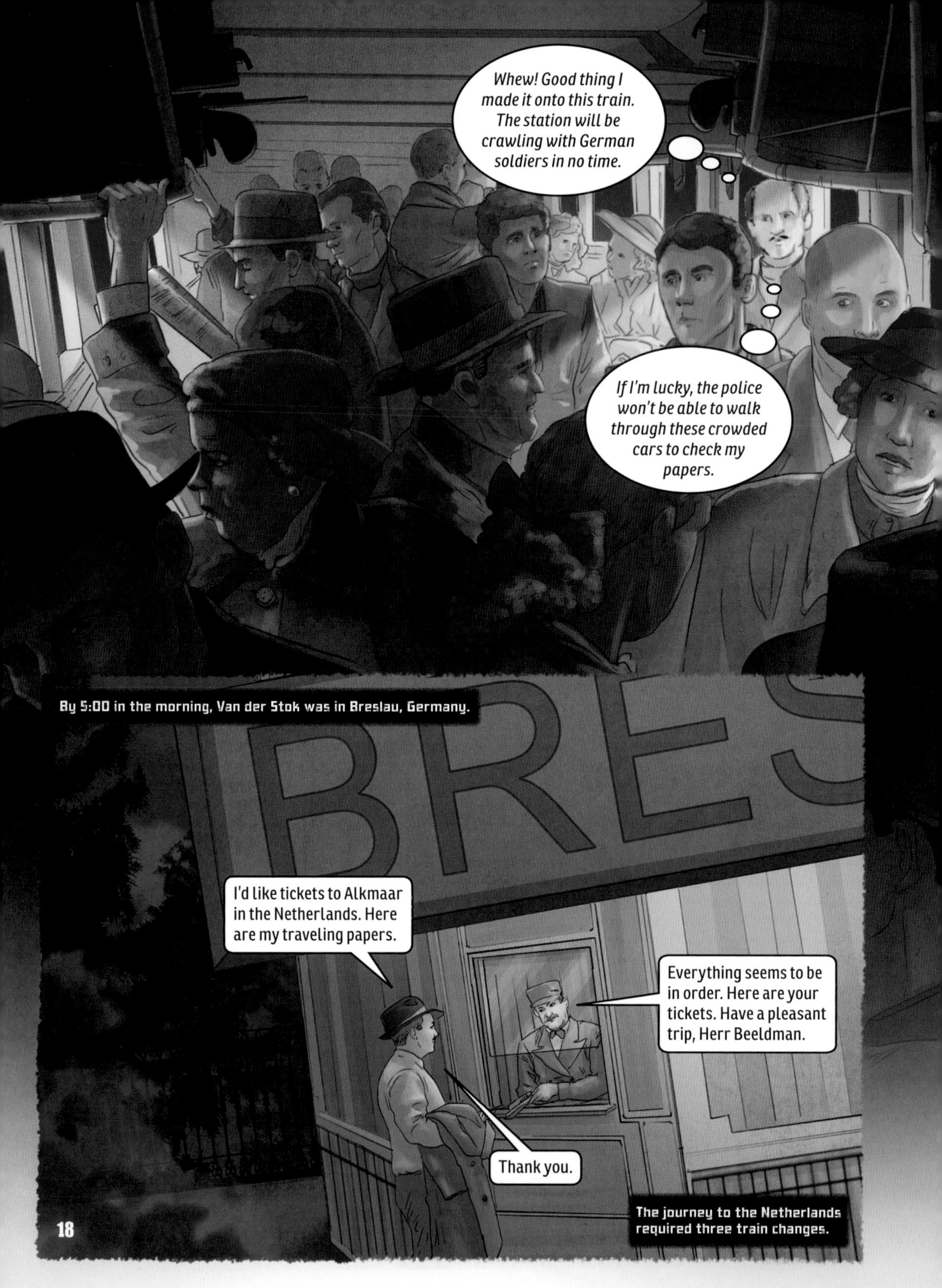
Whew! Good thing I made it onto this train. The station will be crawling with German soldiers in no time.
If I'm lucky, the police won't be able to walk through these crowded cars to check my papers.
By 5:00 in the morning, Van der Stok was in Breslau, Germany.
BRES
I'd like tickets to Alkmaar in the Netherlands. Here are my traveling papers.
Everything seems to be in order. Here are your tickets. Have a pleasant trip, Herr Beeldman.
Thank you.
The journey to the Netherlands required three train changes.

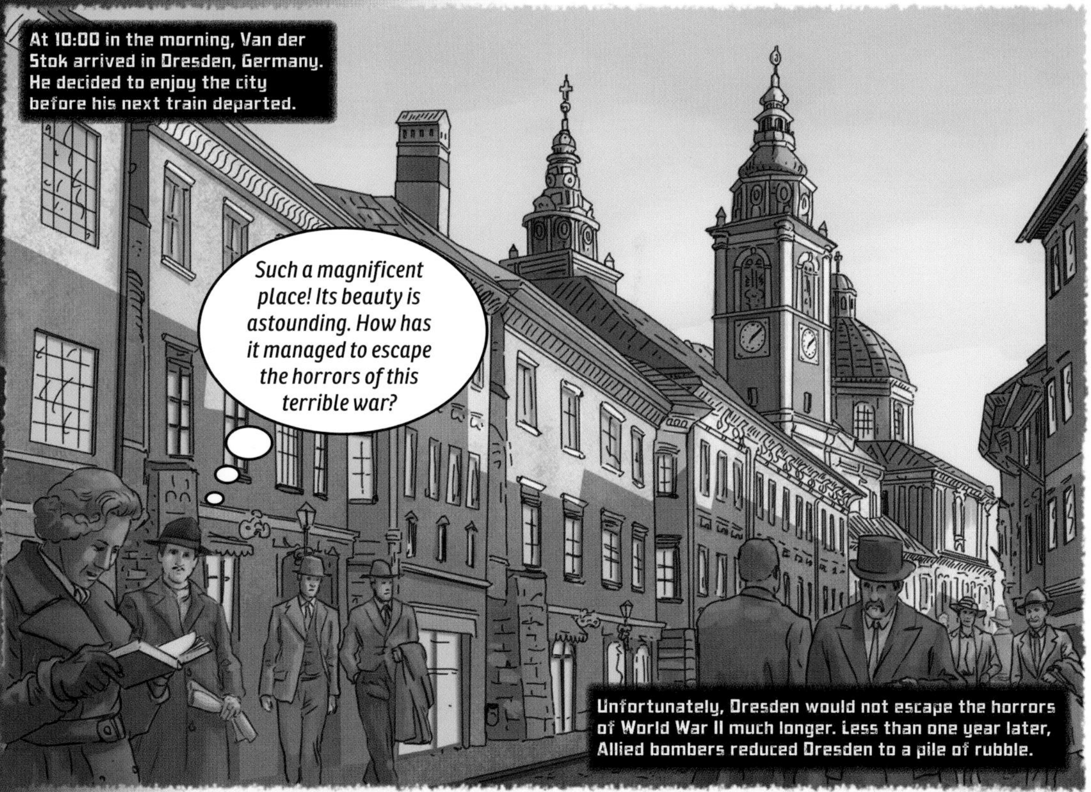
At 10:00 in the morning, Van der Stok arrived in Dresden, Germany. He decided to enjoy the city before his next train departed.
Such a magnificent place! Its beauty is astounding. How has it managed to escape the horrors of this terrible war?
Unfortunately, Dresden would not escape the horrors of World War II much longer. Less than one year later, Allied bombers reduced Dresden to a pile of rubble.

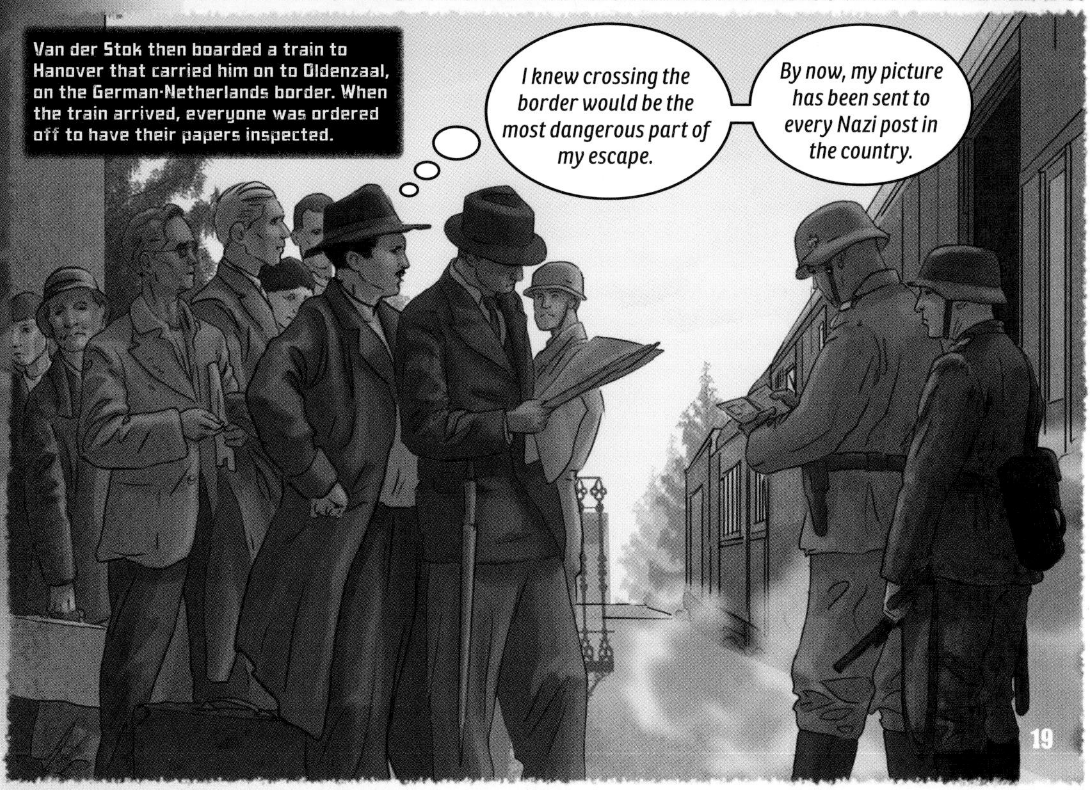
Van der Stok then boarded a train to Hanover that carried him on to Oldenzaal, on the German-Netherlands border. When the train arrived, everyone was ordered off to have their papers inspected.
I knew crossing the border would be the most dangerous part of my escape.
By now, my picture has been sent to every Nazi post in the country.

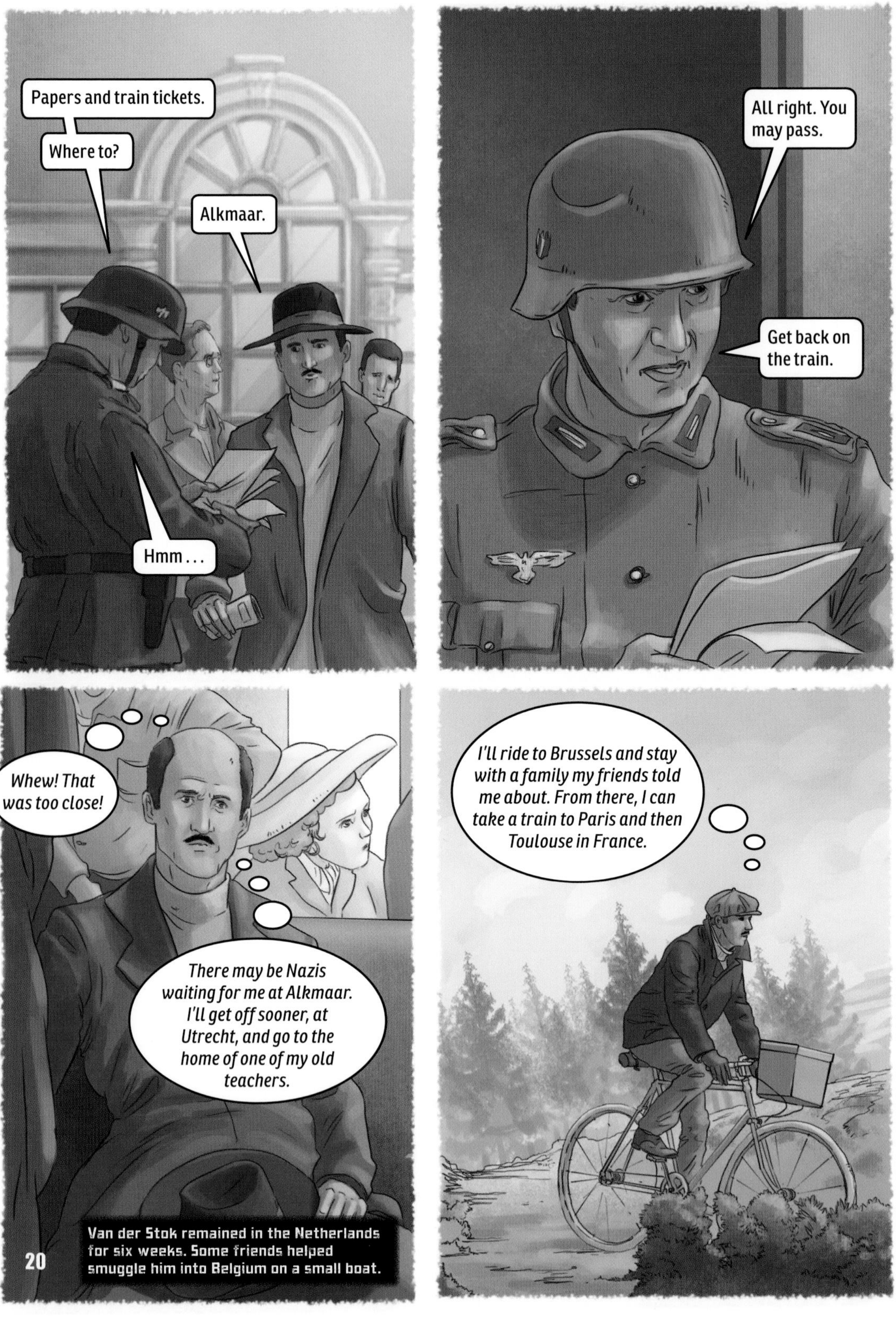
Papers and train tickets.
Where to?
Alkmaar.
Hmm . . .
All right. You may pass.
Get back on the train.
Whew! That was too close!
There may be Nazis waiting for me at Alkmaar. I'll get off sooner, at Utrecht, and go to the home of one of my old teachers.
Van der Stok remained in the Netherlands for six weeks. Some friends helped smuggle him into Belgium on a small boat.
I'll ride to Brussels and stay with a family my friends told me about. From there, I can take a train to Paris and then Toulouse in France.

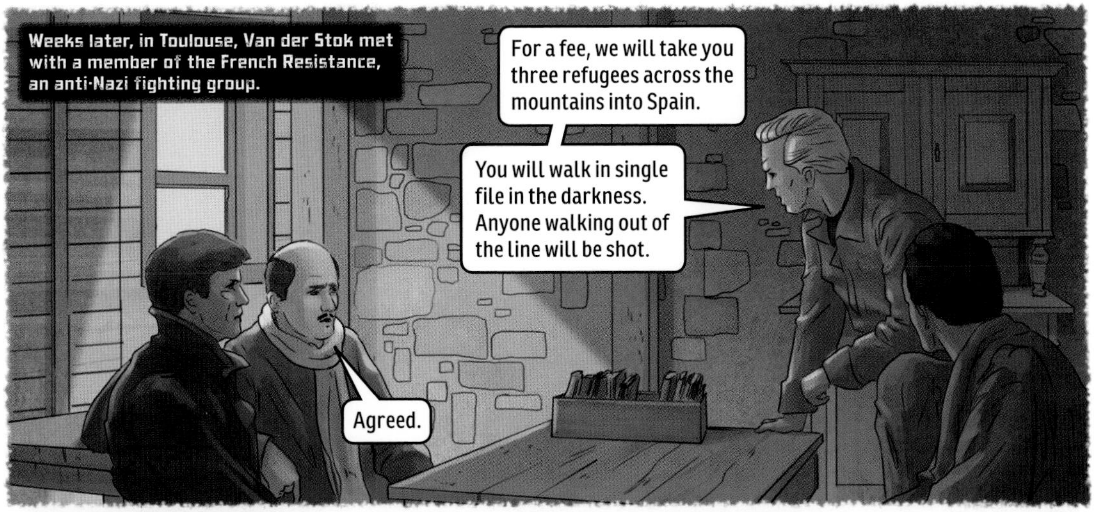
Weeks later, in Toulouse, Van der Stok met with a member of the French Resistance, an anti-Nazi fighting group.
For a fee, we will take you three refugees across the mountains into Spain.
You will walk in single file in the darkness. Anyone walking out of the line will be shot.
Agreed.

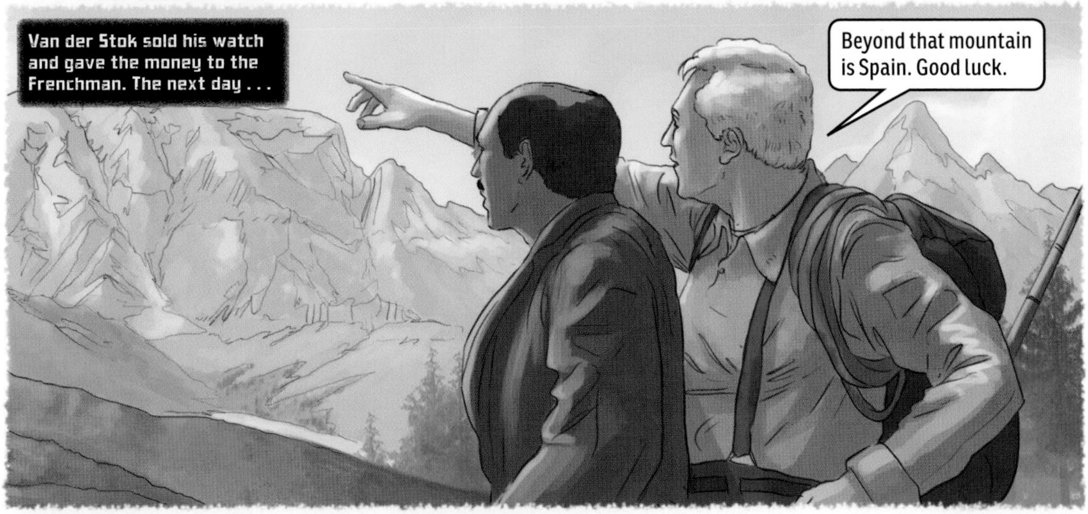
Van der Stok sold his watch and gave the money to the Frenchman. The next day . . .
Beyond that mountain is Spain. Good luck.

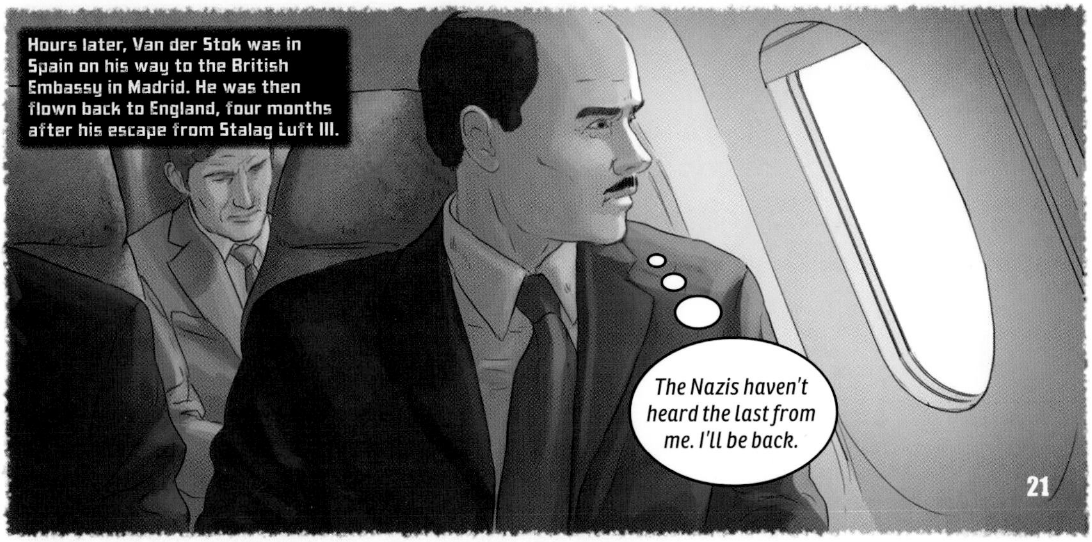
Hours later, Van der Stok was in Spain on his way to the British Embassy in Madrid. He was then flown back to England, four months after his escape from Stalag Luft III.
The Nazis haven't heard the last from me. I'll be back.

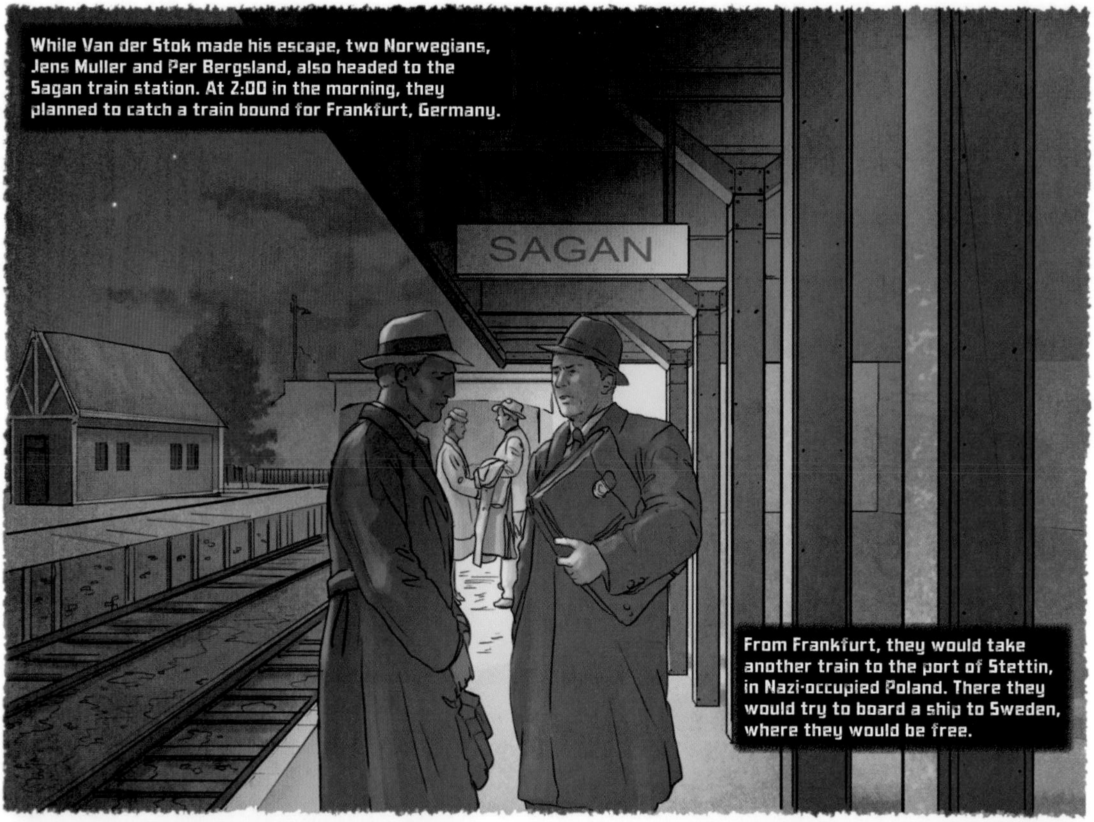
While Van der Stok made his escape, two Norwegians, Jens Muller and Per Bergsland, also headed to the Sagan train station. At 2:00 in the morning, they planned to catch a train bound for Frankfurt, Germany.
SAGAN
From Frankfurt, they would take another train to the port of Stettin, in Nazi-occupied Poland. There they would try to board a ship to Sweden, where they would be free.

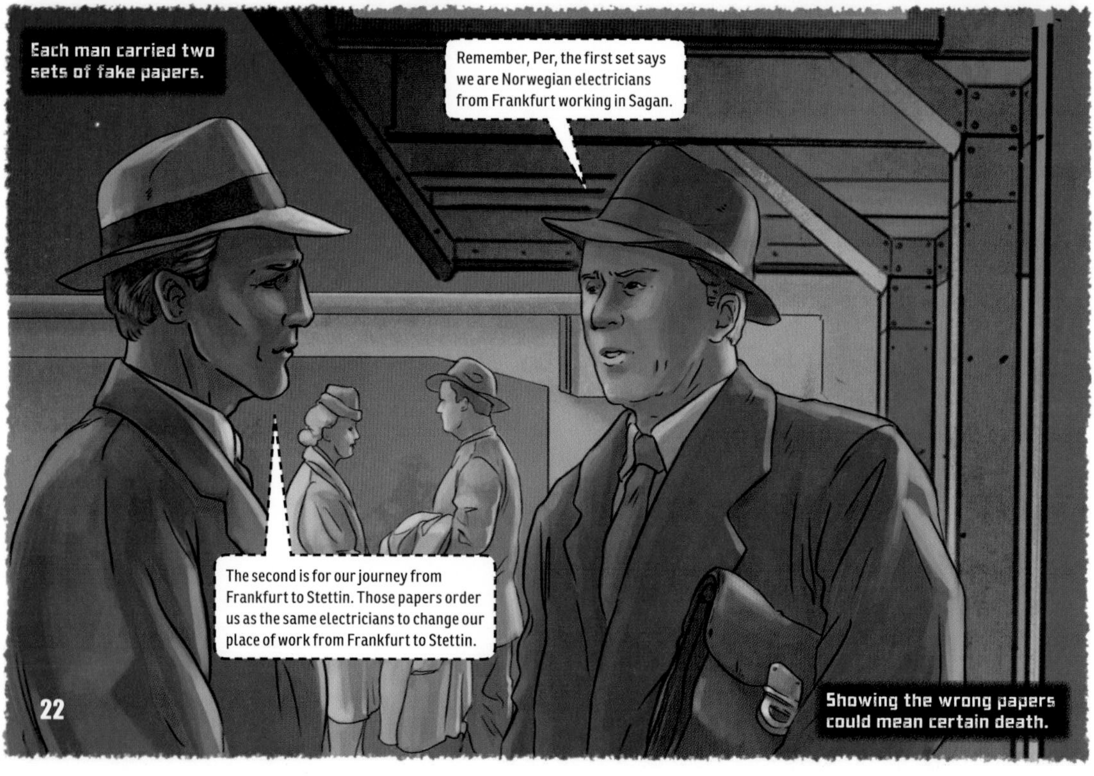
Each man carried two sets of fake papers.
Remember, Per, the first set says we are Norwegian electricians from Frankfurt working in Sagan.
The second is for our journey from Frankfurt to Stettin. Those papers order us as the same electricians to change our place of work from Frankfurt to Stettin.
Showing the wrong papers could mean certain death.

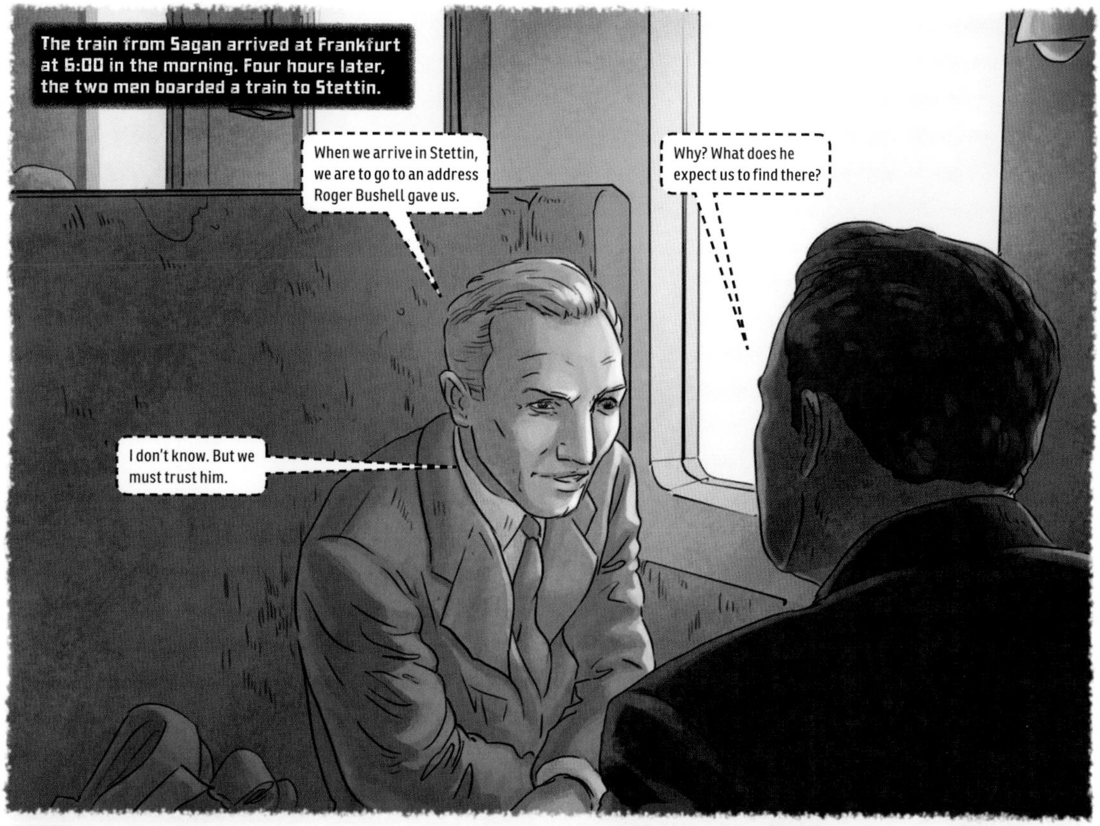
The train from Sagan arrived at Frankfurt at 6:00 in the morning. Four hours later, the two men boarded a train to Stettin.
When we arrive in Stettin, we are to go to an address Roger Bushell gave us.
Why? What does he expect us to find there?
I don't know. But we must trust him.

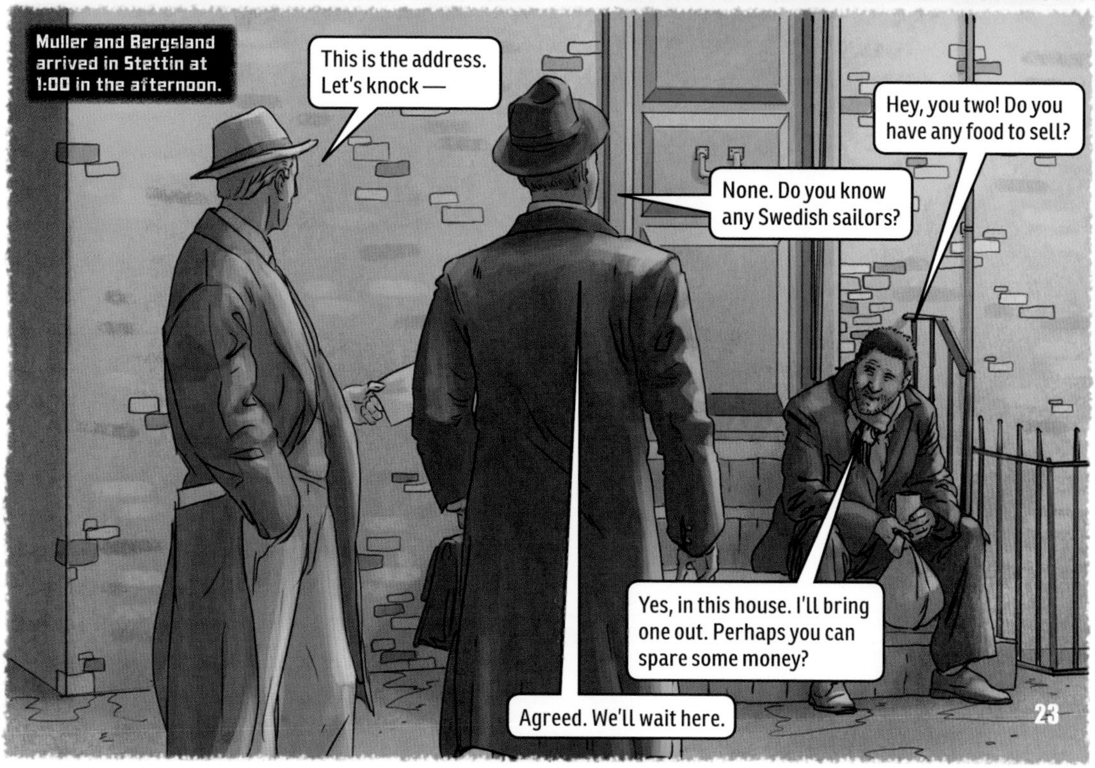
Muller and Bergsland arrived in Stettin at 1:00 in the afternoon.
This is the address. Let's knock —
Hey, you two! Do you have any food to sell?
None. Do you know any Swedish sailors?
Yes, in this house. I'll bring one out. Perhaps you can spare some money?
Agreed. We'll wait here.

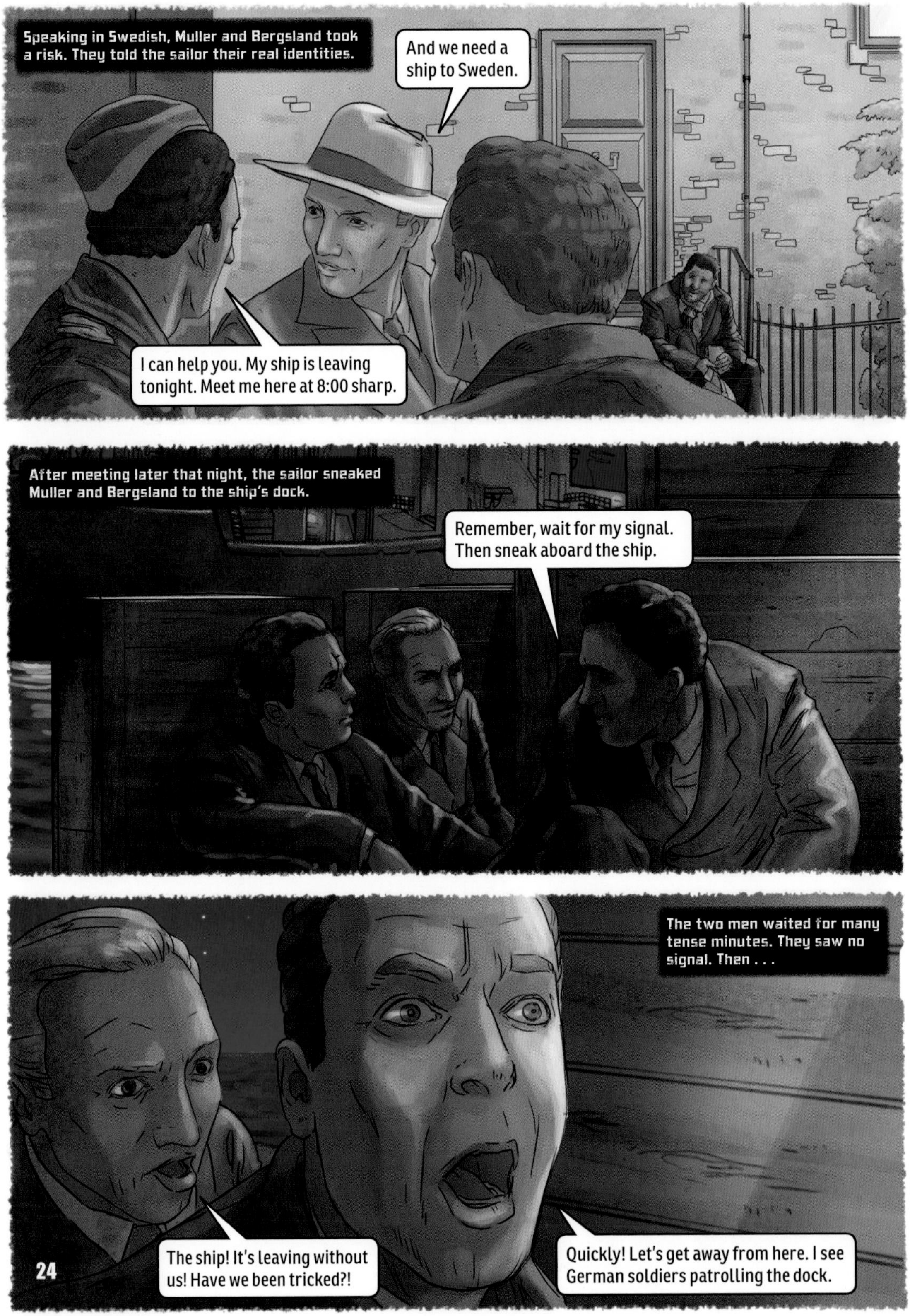

Speaking in Swedish, Muller and Bergsland took a risk. They told the sailor their real identities.
And we need a ship to Sweden.
I can help you. My ship is leaving tonight. Meet me here at 8:00 sharp.
After meeting later that night, the sailor sneaked Muller and Bergsland to the ship's dock.
Remember, wait for my signal. Then sneak aboard the ship.
The two men waited for many tense minutes. They saw no signal. Then . . .
The ship! It's leaving without us! Have we been tricked?!
Quickly! Let's get away from here. I see German soldiers patrolling the dock.

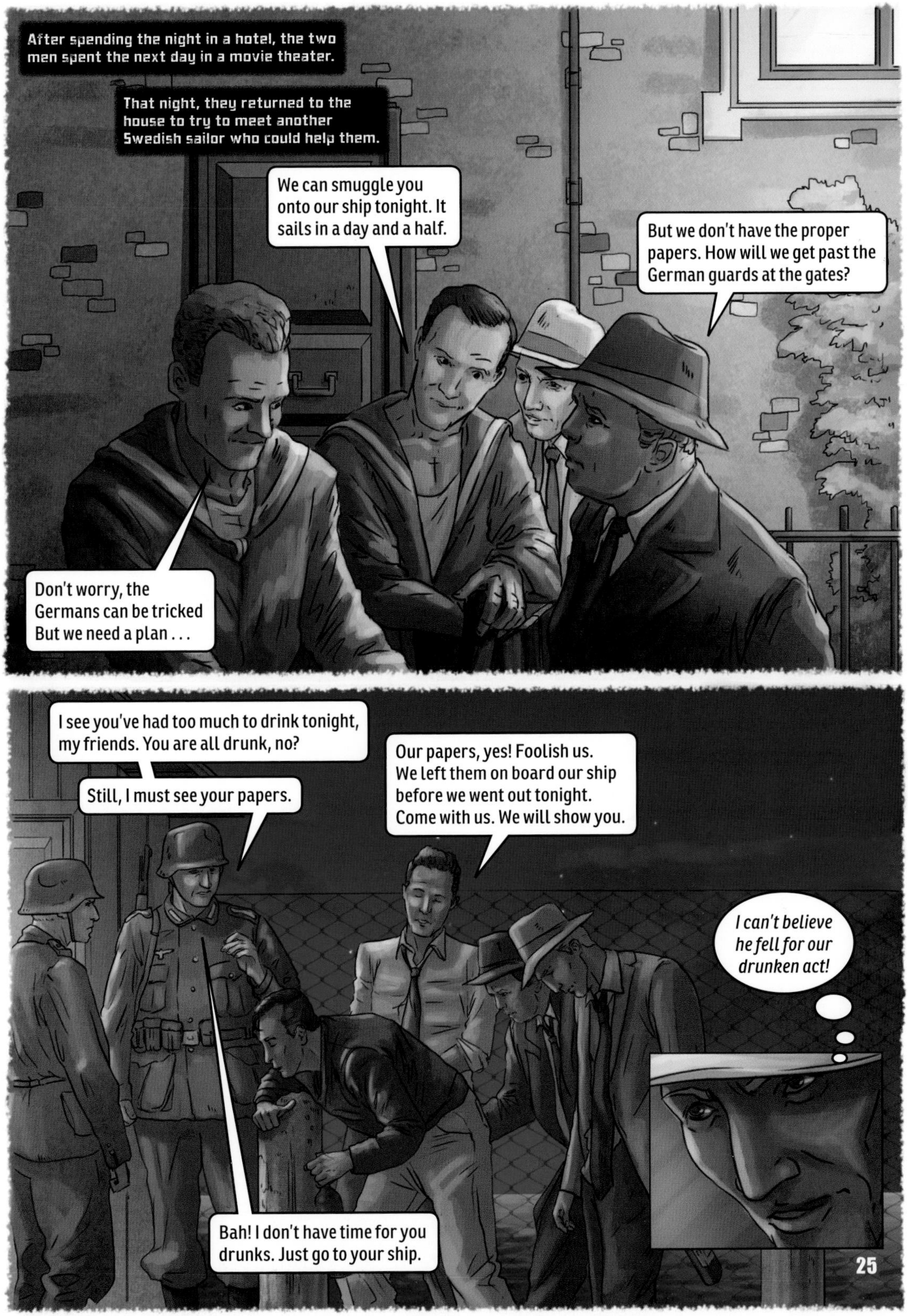
After spending the night in a hotel, the two men spent the next day in a movie theater.
That night, they returned to the house to try to meet another Swedish sailor who could help them.
We can smuggle you onto our ship tonight. It sails in a day and a half.
But we don't have the proper papers. How will we get past the German guards at the gates?
Don't worry, the Germans can be tricked But we need a plan . . .
I see you've had too much to drink tonight, my friends. You are all drunk, no?
Still, I must see your papers.
Our papers, yes! Foolish us. We left them on board our ship before we went out tonight. Come with us. We will show you.
I can't believe he fell for our drunken act!
Bah! I don't have time for you drunks. Just go to your ship.

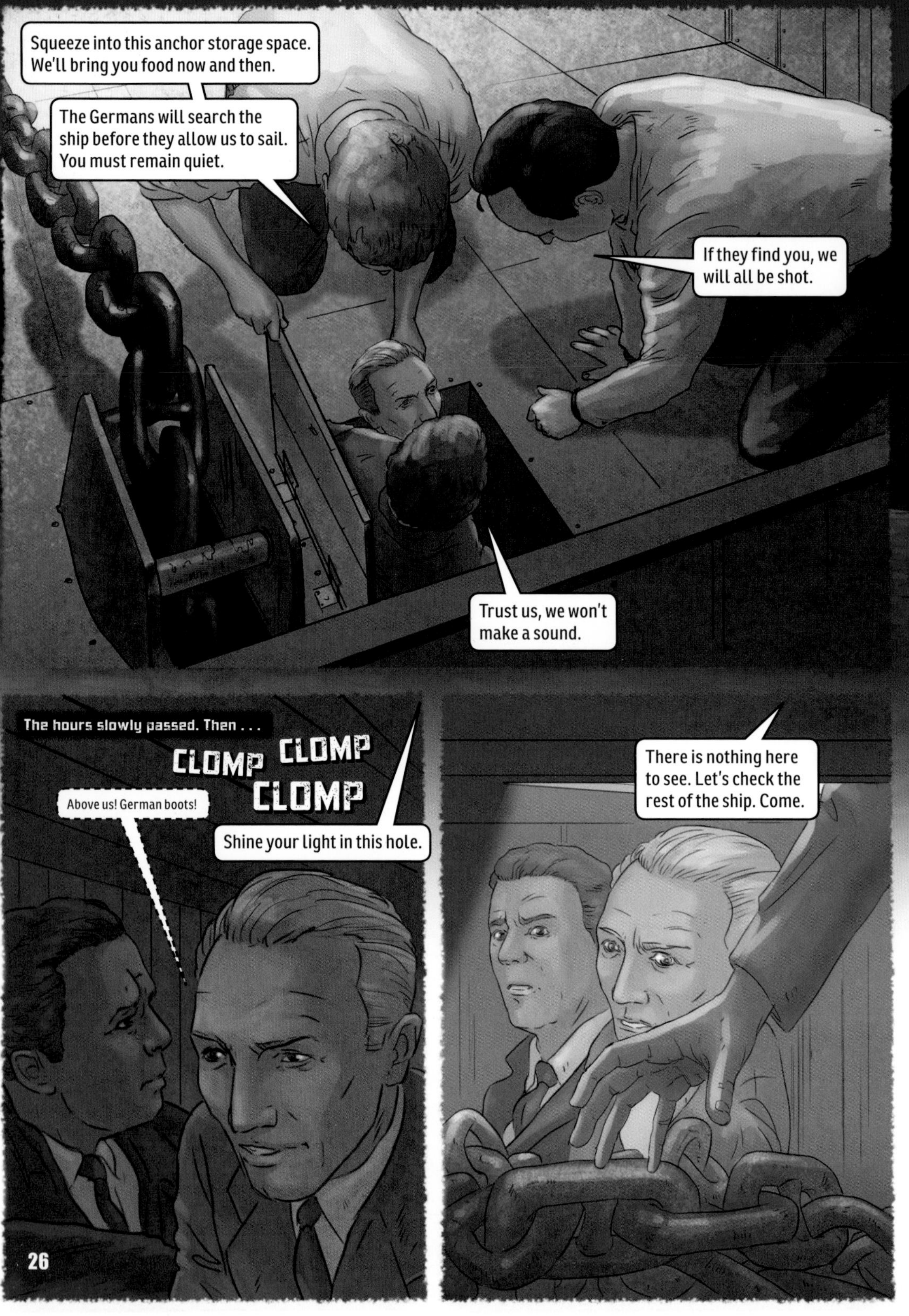
Squeeze into this anchor storage space. We'll bring you food now and then.
The Germans will search the ship before they allow us to sail. You must remain quiet.
If they find you, we will all be shot.
Trust us, we won't make a sound.
The hours slowly passed. Then . . .
CLOMP CLOMP
CLOMP
Above us! German boots!
Shine your light in this hole.
There is nothing here to see. Let's check the rest of the ship. Come.

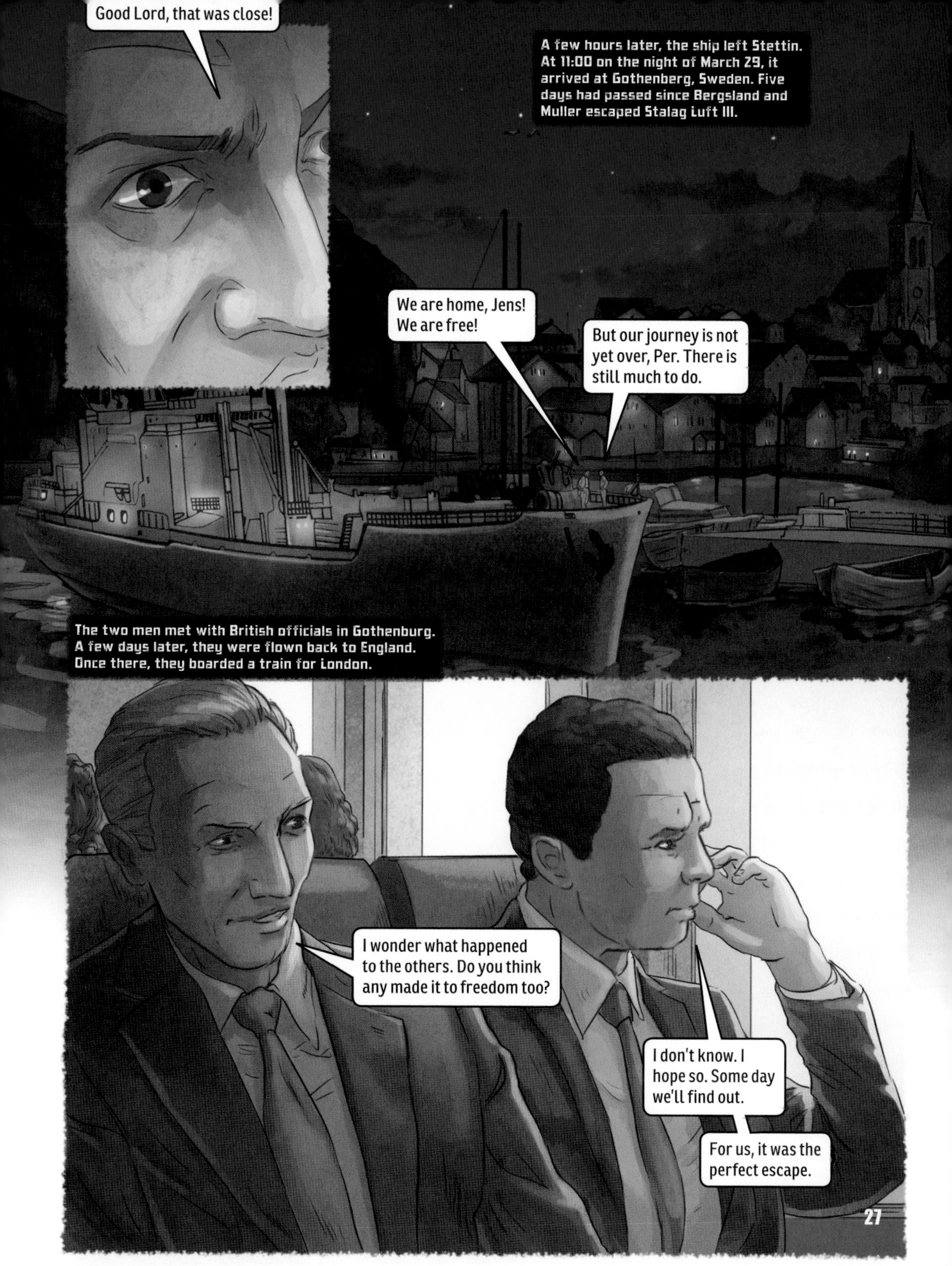

Good Lord, that was close!
A few hours later, the ship left Stettin. At 11:00 on the night of March 29, it arrived at Gothenberg, Sweden. Five days had passed since Bergsland and Muller escaped Stalag Luft III.
We are home, Jens! We are free!
But our journey is not yet over, Per. There is still much to do.
The two men met with British officials in Gothenburg. A few days later, they were flown back to England. Once there, they boarded a train for London.
I wonder what happened to the others. Do you think any made it to freedom too?
I don't know. I hope so. Some day we'll find out.
For us, it was the perfect escape.

HEROES ALL

T hough only three of the 76 escapees reached freedom, the breakout from Stalag Luft III achieved its main goal. Thousands, if not millions, of German civilians, police, and military personnel were tied up hunting for the escapees for many weeks. Their efforts prevented them from doing their more important work to help the Nazi war effort.

Back in England, Bob Van der Stok rejoined the British air force. He flew Spitfire fighters in Operation Overlord, the code name for D-Day, or the invasion of Western Europe in June 1944. The following year he was placed in command of a Dutch squadron in the Netherlands. There he learned that his two brothers had been killed in concentration camps and the Nazis had blinded his father.

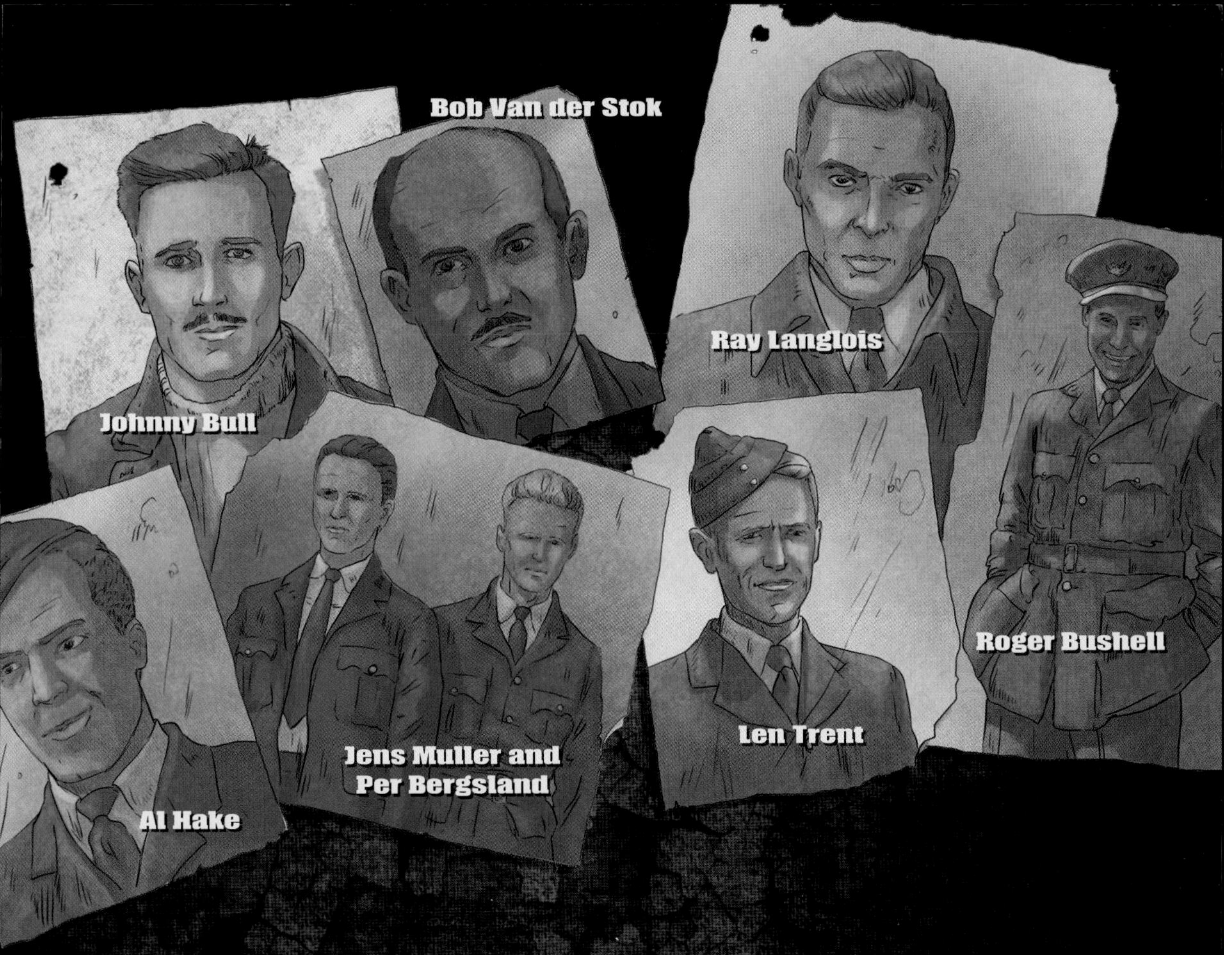
Bob Van der Stok
Ray Langlois
Johnny Bull
Roger Bushell
Len Trent
Jens Muller and
Per Bergsland
Al Hake

After the war, Van der Stok moved to the United States and worked for the National Aeronautics and Space Administration (NASA) and the U.S. Coast Guard. He died in 1993 at age 78.

Per Bergsland and Jens Muller went to Canada for the rest of the war. After the conflict, both men worked for Norwegian airlines companies. Bergsland died in 1992 at age 74. Muller died in 1999 at age 82.

Today the escape from Stalag Luft III is known as The Great Escape. Everyone involved — the planners, the diggers, the watchmen, the forgers, the tailors, and many more — contributed to this legendary flight to freedom. They are heroes all!

GLOSSARY

airman (AYR-man)—a person in the Air Force

air raid (AYR RAYD)—an attack in which bombs are dropped from aircraft onto a ground target

Allied forces (AL-lyd FORSS-ess)—countries united against Germany during World War II, including France, the United States, Canada, Great Britain, and others

barracks (BAR-uhks)—a building where soldiers are housed

concentration camp (kahn-suhn-TRAY-shuhn KAMP)—a prison camp where thousands of inmates are held under harsh conditions

destination (des-tuh-NAY-shuhn)—the place to which one is traveling

escapee (ess-kape-EE)—a person who has escaped

forgery (FOR-jur-ee)—an illegal copy of something, such as a document

Nazi (NOT-see)—a member of the National Socialist Party led by Adolf Hitler that controlled Germany before and during World War II

refugee (ref-yuh-JEE)—a person forced to leave his or her home because of natural disaster or war

resistance (ri-ZISS-tuhnss)—fighting back

smuggle (SMUHG-uhl)—to bring something or someone into or out of a country illegally

CRITICAL THINKING USING THE COMMON CORE

1. Make a list of the skills you think the prisoners required to make the escape. As you do, consider all stages of the breakout, including planning, digging, forging, and other phases of work. (Key Ideas and Details)

2. This book begins with narrative text, changes to comic book storytelling, and ends with narrative text. Why did the author set up the book this way? How does this structure help you better understand the story? (Craft and Structure)

3. Assume the identity of a prisoner in a Stalag Luft during World War II. Write a journal entry telling your experiences from your point of view. Describe your job as an Allied airmen, your capture by the Germans, life in the camp, your decision to participate in the breakout or not, and other details. (Key Ideas and Details)

READ MORE

Chandler, Matt. *Behind Enemy Lines: The Escape of Robert Grimes with the Comet Line.* Great Escapes of World War II. North Mankato, Minn.: Capstone Press, 2017.

Guillain, Charlotte. *Great Escapes.* War Stories. Chicago: Heinemann Library, 2012.

Sherman, Jill. *Eyewitness to the Liberation of Buchenwald.* Eyewitness to World War II. Mankato, Minn.: Childs World, 2016.

Woolf, Alex. *Children of the Holocaust.* Hauppauge, N.Y.: Barron's, 2014.

INTERNET SITES

FactHound offers a safe, fun way to find Internet sites related to this book. All sites on FactHound have been researched by our staff.

Here's all you do:

Visit *www.facthound.com*

Type in this code: 9781515735311

Super-cool stuff! Check out projects, games and lots more at
www.capstonekids.com

INDEX

TITLES IN THIS SET

BEHIND ENEMY LINES:
The Escape of Robert Grimes with the Comet Line

DEATH CAMP UPRISING:
The Escape from Sobibor Concentration Camp

OUTRUNNING THE NAZIS:
The Brave Escape of Resistance Fighter Sven Somme

TUNNELING TO FREEDOM:
The Great Escape from Stalag Luft III